EXERCISES IN ENGLISH

☆ **GRAMMAR FOR LIFE** ☆

TEACHER'S EDITION

LEVEL E

LOYOLAPRESS.

CHICAGO

The Complete Grammar Program with Character

Enhancing Grammar with Grade-Level Science, Social Studies, Language Arts, and Character Education

- **Instruction** and **practice** in every area of modern grammar, usage, and mechanics help students build comprehensive, lifelong skills.

- **Grade-level science**, **social studies**, and **language arts** content reinforces learning in other subject areas.

- **Character education** enriches students' lives through profiles of multicultural role models.

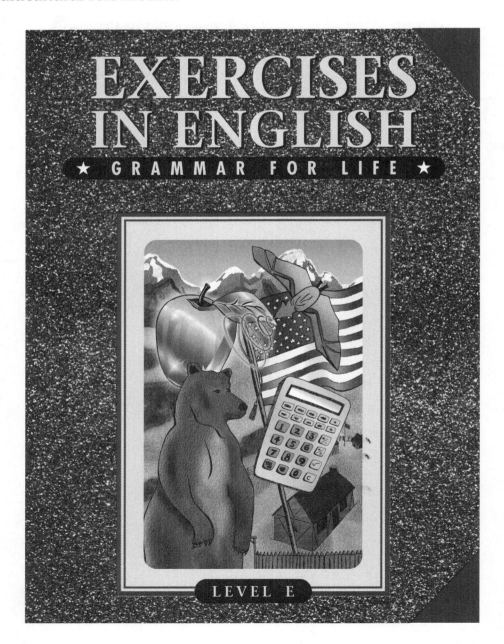

EXERCISES IN ENGLISH
★ GRAMMAR FOR LIFE ★

ED'S

LEVEL

EXERCISES IN ENGLISH
★ GRAMMAR FOR LIFE ★

VEL D

EXERCISES IN ENGLISH
★ GRAMMAR FOR LIFE ★

LEVEL F

EXERC
IN EN
★ GRAMMAR

LEVEL G

ERCISES
ENGLISH
RAMMAR FOR LIFE ★

LEVEL H

A Six-Level Program

Carefully sequenced Student Editions for grades 3–8 provide thorough teaching of all modern grammar concepts.

Easy-to-use Teacher's Editions offer clear, concise answers to exercises.

Introductory Review section, starting at Level D, helps students get back on track at the beginning of the year.

Self-teaching student lessons optimize class time.

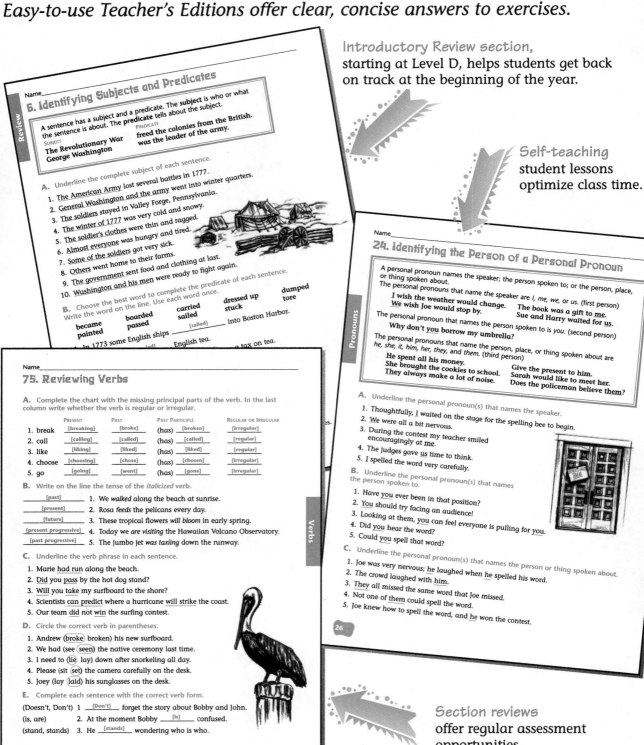

Review

Name_____

6. Identifying Subjects and Predicates

A sentence has a subject and a predicate. The **subject** is who or what the sentence is about. The **predicate** tells about the subject.

SUBJECT
The Revolutionary War
George Washington

PREDICATE
freed the colonies from the British.
was the leader of the army.

A. Underline the complete subject of each sentence.

1. The American Army lost several battles in 1777.
2. General Washington and the army went into winter quarters.
3. The soldiers stayed in Valley Forge, Pennsylvania.
4. The winter of 1777 was very cold and snowy.
5. The soldier's clothes were thin and ragged.
6. Almost everyone was hungry and tired.
7. Some of the soldiers got very sick.
8. Others went home to their farms.
9. The government sent food and clothing at last.
10. Washington and his men were ready to fight again.

B. Choose the best word to complete the predicate of each sentence. Write the word on the line. Use each word once.

became   boarded   carried   dressed up   dumped
painted   passed   sailed   stuck   tore

__[sailed]__ into Boston Harbor.

1. In 1773 some English ships English tea.

a tax on tea.

Name_____

75. Reviewing Verbs

A. Complete the chart with the missing principal parts of the verb. In the last column write whether the verb is regular or irregular.

	PRESENT	PAST	PAST PARTICIPLE		REGULAR OR IRREGULAR
1.	break	[breaking]	[broke]	(has) [broken]	[Irregular]
2.	call	[calling]	[called]	(has) [called]	[regular]
3.	like	[liking]	[liked]	(has) [liked]	[regular]
4.	choose	[choosing]	[chose]	(has) [chosen]	[Irregular]
5.	go	[going]	[went]	(has) [gone]	[irregular]

B. Write on the line the tense of the *italicized* verb.

__[past]__ 1. We *walked* along the beach at sunrise.
__[present]__ 2. Rosa *feeds* the pelicans every day.
__[future]__ 3. These tropical flowers *will bloom* in early spring.
__[present progressive]__ 4. Today we *are visiting* the Hawaiian Volcano Observatory.
__[past progressive]__ 5. The jumbo jet *was taxiing* down the runway.

C. Underline the verb phrase in each sentence.

1. Marie had run along the beach.
2. Did you pass by the hot dog stand?
3. Will you take my surfboard to the shore?
4. Scientists can predict where a hurricane will strike the coast.
5. Our team did not win the surfing contest.

D. Circle the correct verb in parentheses.

1. Andrew (broke) broken) his new surfboard.
2. We had (see (seen) the native ceremony last time.
3. I need to (lie) lay) down after snorkeling all day.
4. Please (sit (set) the camera carefully on the desk.
5. Joey (lay (laid) his sunglasses on the desk.

E. Complete each sentence with the correct verb form.

(Doesn't, Don't) 1 __[Don't]__ forget the story about Bobby and John.
(is, are) 2. At the moment Bobby __[is]__ confused.
(stand, stands) 3. He __[stands]__ wondering who is who.

CONTINUED **79**

Verbs

Pronouns

Name_____

24. Identifying the Person of a Personal Pronoun

A personal pronoun names the speaker; the person spoken to; or the person, place, or thing spoken about.

The personal pronouns that name the speaker are *I, me, we,* or *us.* (first person)

I wish the weather would change.   The book was a gift to me.
We wish Joe would stop by.   Sue and Harry waited for us.

The personal pronoun that names the person spoken to is *you.* (second person)

Why don't you borrow my umbrella?

The personal pronouns that name the person, place, or thing spoken about are *he, she, it, him, her, they,* and *them.* (third person)

He spent all his money.   Give the present to him.
She brought the cookies to school. Sarah would like to meet her.
They always make a lot of noise.   Does the policeman believe them?

A. Underline the personal pronoun(s) that names the speaker.

1. Thoughtfully, I waited on the stage for the spelling bee to begin.
2. We were all a bit nervous.
3. During the contest my teacher smiled encouragingly at me.
4. The judges gave us time to think.
5. I spelled the word very carefully.

B. Underline the personal pronoun(s) that names the person spoken to.

1. Have you ever been in that position?
2. You should try facing an audience!
3. Looking at them, you can feel everyone is pulling for you.
4. Did you hear the word?
5. Could you spell that word?

C. Underline the personal pronoun(s) that names the person or thing spoken about.

1. Joe was very nervous; he laughed when he spelled his word.
2. The crowd laughed with him.
3. They all missed the same word that Joe missed.
4. Not one of them could spell the word.
5. Joe knew how to spell the word, and he won the contest.

26

Section reviews offer regular assessment opportunities.

Features that set us apart...

Clear definitions and examples
help students easily understand concepts.

80. Comparing with Adverbs

Many adverbs have three **degrees of comparison**: positive, comparative, and superlative.
The comparative of most adverbs that end in -ly is formed by adding *more* or *less* before the positive.
The superlative is formed by adding *most* or *least* before the positive.

| quickly | more quickly | most quickly |
| sadly | less sadly | least sadly |

The comparative of adverbs that don't end in -ly is formed by adding -er.
The superlative is formed by adding -est.

| soon | sooner | soonest |
| far | farther | farthest |

Nouns

Read each sentence. Write **DO** on the line if the *italicized* word is a direct object. Write **SC** if it is a subject complement.

[SC] 1. Tropical rain forests are the earth's oldest living *ecosystems*.
[DO] 2. Rain forests cover only a small *part* of the earth's surface.
[SC] 3. They are *home* to half the plant and animal species on the earth.
[DO] 4. Rain falls up to eight *meters* a year.
[DO] 5. Rain forests have no dry or cold *seasons*.
[DO] 6. A tropical rain forest has four *layers*.
[SC] 7. The emergent layer is the highest *layer* in a rain forest.
[DO] 8. The canopy contains the *tops* of the tallest trees.
[DO] 9. The emergent layer and the canopy receive the most *sunshine*.
[SC] 10. Most rain forest animals are *inhabitants* of the top layers.
[SC] 11. The fourth layer of a rain forest is the *understory*.
[DO] 12. Tree roots, soil, and decaying material make up the forest *floor*.
[DO] 13. The understory and the forest floor receive very little *light*.
[SC] 14. Large animals are *residents* of the forest floor.
[SC] 15. Foods such as bananas, chocolate, and pepper are *products* of rain forests.
[SC] 16. These foods are maintainable *resources*.
[DO] 17. The Amazon rain forest covers an *area* about two-thirds the size of the continental United States.
[SC] 18. It is the world's largest rain *forest*.
[DO] 19. Rain forests help control the world's *climate*.
[DO] 20. Rain forests affect *everyone* on Earth.

Grade-level content
provides enrichment and reinforcement of what is being studied in science, social studies, and language arts.

Pronouns

A. Circle the subject pronoun in each sentence.

1. I just read a book about Mathew Brady.
2. You must have heard of him.
3. He was born in Warren County, New York, in 1823.
4. At sixteen, he moved to New York City to study painting.
5. I was surprised at his young age.
6. Soon he started to learn photography.
7. It had just been introduced in the United States.
8. In 1849 he opened a studio in Washington, D.C.
9. He began taking photos of famous people.
10. They all liked his wonderful pictures.

B. Change the *italicized* word(s) in each sentence to a subject pronoun. Write the pronoun on the line. Use a capital letter if necessary.

[It] 1. *The Civil War* began in 1861.
[They] 2. *Brady and a group of photographers* took pictures of the battlefields.
[He] 3. *Brady* shocked the world by exhibiting the photos.
[they] 4. For the first time *ordinary people* saw the horror of war.
[he] 5. Later in his life *Brady* fell on hard times.
[It] 6. *Congress* bought his negatives for $25,000.
[She] 7. *My mother* is a big fan of Brady's pictures.
[We] 8. *My family and I* went to an exhibition of his photographs.
[They] 9. *These pictures* are the best known photographs of the Civil War.
[It] 10. *His work* gives us a visual sense of days gone by.

Mathew Brady was always trying to improve his work. Give an example of how you could improve something in your life (a hobby, a project, a friendship, some schoolwork).

Character education lessons
offer students information on multicultural role models on a consistent basis.

Prepositions, Conjunctions, Interjections

E. Write appropriate interjections on the lines. **[Answers will vary.]**

[Shh!] 1. Mike Fink is aiming for the mosquito on the fence.
[What!] 2. Did Mike jump across the Ohio River?
[Wow!] 3. Those two were amazing.
[Hush!] 4. She's telling the story of another folk hero.
[Great!] 5. I love these stories.

Try It Yourself.
Write three sentences about your favorite folktale character. Use prepositional phrases, conjunctions, and at least one interjection in your sentences.

Check Your Own Work
Choose a selection from your writing portfolio, your journal, a work in progress, an assignment from another class, or a letter. Revise it, applying the skills you have reviewed. The checklist will help you.

✔ Have you used appropriate prepositions?
✔ Have you used *between, among, from,* and *off* correctly?
✔ Have you used interjections that express the correct emotions?

108

Writing in context
allows students to practice and use what they have learned.

Name_____

139. Using an Almanac

Almanacs are fascinating reference books full of facts. Almanacs are published every year and give up-to-date information on a variety of topics. For example, you can find a list of important events in the history of U.S. spaceflight from 1961 to the present. You also can find answers to questions such as What are the 10 largest cities in the United States or in the world?

Almanacs generally have both a contents listing and an index. To find information, decide on a keyword or phrase about your topic and then look for it in the index. For example, if you are interested in rail travel in the United States, you might use **railroads** as your keyword and when you find railroads, then look for **U.S.**

Information in an almanac is often given as a table, chart, or list. There is less background information in an almanac than you will find in an encyclopedia.

The Great Lakes
Source: National Ocean Service, U.S. Dept. of Commerce

The Great Lakes form the world's largest body of fresh water, and with their connecting waterways are the largest inland water transportation unit. Draining the great North Central basin of the U.S., they enable shipping to reach the Gulf of Mexico via the Illinois Waterway, and to reach the Atlantic via their outlet, the St. Lawrence R., and to reach Michigan to the Mississippi R. A 3d outlet connects with the Hudson R. and then the Atlantic via the New York State Barge Canal System. Traffic on the Illinois Waterway and the N.Y. State Barge Canal System is limited to recreational boating and small shipping vessels.

Only one of the lakes, Lake Michigan, is wholly in the U.S.; the others are shared with Canada. Ships move from the shores of Lake Superior to Whitefish Bay at the E end of the lake, then through the Soo (Sault Ste. Marie) locks, through the St. Mary's R. and into Lake Huron. To reach Gary and the Port of Indiana and South Chicago, IL, ships move W from Lake Huron to Lake Michigan through the Straits of Mackinac. Lake Superior is 601 ft above low water datum at Rimouski, Quebec, on the International Great Lakes Datum (1985). From Duluth, MN, to the E end of Lake Ontario is 1,156 mi.

	Superior	Michigan	Huron	Erie	Ontario
	350	307	206	241	193
	160	118	183	57	53
Length in mi	1,333	923	750	210	802
Breadth in mi	2,935	1,180	850	116	393
Deepest soundings in ft	20,600	22,300	9,100	4,980	3,560
Volume of water in cu mi	11,100		13,900	4,930	3,990
Area (sq mi) water surface—U.S.	16,900	45,600	16,200	18,000	15,200
Canada	32,400		35,500	4,720	12,100
Area (sq mi) entire drainage basin—U.S.	81,000	67,900	74,700	32,630	34,850
Canada					
TOTAL AREA (sq mi) U.S. and Canada				569.20	243.30
Low water datum above mean water level at	601.10	577.50	577.50	41° 23 min	43° 11 min
Rimouski, Quebec, avg. level in ft (1985)	46° 25 min	41° 37 min	43° 00 min	42° 52 min	44° 15 min
Latitude, N	49° 00 min	46° 06 min	46° 17 min	78° 51 min	76° 03 min
	84° 22 min	84° 45 min	79° 43 min	83° 29 min	79° 53 min
Longitude, W	92° 06 min	88° 02 min	84° 45 min	260.8	174.6
National boundary line in mi	282.8	None	580	251.5	300
United States shoreline (mainland only) mi	863	1,400		431	

CONTINUED **151**

E

exclamation point A punctuation mark (!) used after an exclamatory sentence and after an exclamatory word or phrase: More than one thousand people attended the wedding. Wonderful! What a celebration!

H

homophones Words that sound alike but may be spelled differently and have different meanings: *sea* and *see*, *blue* and *blew*.

I

intensive pronoun An intensive pronoun ends in *-self* or *-selves*. The intensive pronouns are

myself   ourselves
yourself   yourselves
himself   themselves
herself
itself

Intensive pronouns are used for emphasis: She *herself* paid the bill.

interjection A word that expresses a strong feeling or emotion. An interjection is followed by an exclamation point: *Ouch! What! Oh!*

N

noun The name of a person, place, or thing.

There are two main kinds of nouns: proper nouns and common nouns.
- A common noun names any one member of a group of persons, places, or things: *queen, city, church.*
- A proper noun names a particular person, place, or thing. A proper noun is capitalized: *Queen Elizabeth, London, Westminster Abbey.*

A noun can be singular or plural.
- A singular noun names one person, place, or thing: *boy, river, berry.*
- A plural noun names more than one person, place, or thing: *boys, rivers, berries.*

(continued on next page)

163

Research Skills section provides teaching and practice with tools such as the Internet and atlases. Students learn to combine grammar and writing in projects for other classes.

Handbook of Terms helps students refresh and expand their knowledge of grammar points.

Sentence Diagramming section, starting at Level D, helps students visually portray the parts of a sentence to better understand and remember concepts.

B. This simple sentence has a subject complement. Indicate a subject complement by drawing a slanted line pointing back to the subject between the verb and the complement. Remember that the complement can be a noun, a pronoun, or an adjective.

Mrs. Mitchell is a good teacher.

C. This simple sentence has a compound subject. Subjects must always appear on horizontal lines. Place the subject on parallel lines and write the conjunction on a broken line between the words it joins.

Tom and Pepe played tennis yesterday.

D. This simple sentence has a compound verb. Indicate a compound verb the same way as a compound subject.

Ned raked and bagged the leaves.

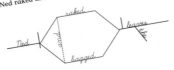

CONTINUED **157**

Plus

- **Flexible format** allows use of the books at multiple grade levels.

- **Perforated student pages** facilitate grading and inclusion in student portfolios.

- **Easy-to-grade exercises** are always divisible by five.

- **Sentence Analysis section** in the Teacher's Edition provides extra tools for daily oral grammar activities.

Exercises in English—Scope and Sequence

SENTENCES	C	D	E	F	G	H
The Four Kinds of Sentences	✔	✔	✔	✔	✔	✔
Subjects and Predicates	✔	✔	✔	✔	✔	✔
Simple Subjects and Predicates		✔		✔	✔	✔
Compound Subjects and Predicates		✔	✔	✔	✔	✔
Direct Objects		✔	✔	✔	✔	✔
Complete Subjects and Predicates			✔	✔	✔	✔
Natural and Inverted Order in Sentences			✔	✔	✔	✔
Indirect Objects				✔	✔	✔
Compound Sentences				✔	✔	✔
Complex Sentences					✔	✔
Compound Complex Sentences						✔
NOUNS	C	D	E	F	G	H
Proper and Common Nouns	✔	✔	✔	✔	✔	✔
Singular and Plural Nouns	✔	✔	✔	✔	✔	✔
Possessive Nouns	✔	✔	✔	✔	✔	✔
Nouns Used as Subjects		✔	✔	✔		
Nouns Used as Objects		✔	✔	✔	✔	✔
Nouns Used as Subject Complements			✔	✔	✔	
Nouns Used in Direct Address			✔	✔		
Nouns Used as Objects of Prepositions			✔	✔	✔	
Appositives				✔	✔	
Collective Nouns				✔	✔	✔
Concrete and Abstract Nouns				✔	✔	✔
Words Used as Nouns and Verbs				✔		✔
Nouns Used as Object Complements						✔
VERBS	C	D	E	F	G	H
Regular and Irregular Verbs	✔	✔	✔	✔	✔	✔
Present Tense	✔	✔	✔	✔	✔	✔
Progressive Tenses	✔	✔	✔	✔	✔	✔
Past Tense	✔	✔	✔	✔	✔	✔
Future Tenses	✔	✔	✔	✔	✔	✔
Action Verbs	✔	✔	✔			
Verbs of Being	✔	✔	✔			
Helping Verbs	✔	✔				
Forms of *Bring*	✔					
Forms of *Buy*	✔					

Forms of *Come*	✔					
Forms of *Eat*	✔					
Forms of *Go*	✔		✔			
Forms of *See*	✔		✔			
Forms of *Sit* and *Set*	✔		✔	✔		
Forms of *Take*	✔		✔			
Forms of *Write*	✔					
Forms of *To Be*	✔	✔	✔			
Forms of *Begin*		✔				
Forms of *Break*		✔	✔			
Forms of *Choose*		✔	✔			
Forms of *Do*		✔				
Verb Phrases		✔	✔	✔	✔	
Intransitive Verbs (Linking Verbs)		✔	✔	✔	✔	✔
There Is and *There Are*		✔		✔	✔	
Subject-Verb Agreement			✔	✔	✔	✔
Transitive Verbs			✔	✔	✔	✔
Doesn't and *Don't*			✔	✔	✔	✔
Let and *Leave*			✔	✔		
Teach and *Learn*			✔			
Lie and *Lay*			✔	✔		
Rise and *Raise*				✔		
Perfect Tenses				✔	✔	
Words Used as Nouns and Verbs					✔	
Active and Passive Voice					✔	✔
Modal Auxiliary Verbs					✔	✔
You Are and *You Were*					✔	
Compound Tenses						✔
Emphatic Verb Forms						✔
PRONOUNS	C	D	E	F	G	H
Singular and Plural Pronouns	✔	✔	✔			
Subject Pronouns	✔	✔	✔	✔	✔	✔
Possessive Pronouns	✔	✔	✔	✔	✔	✔
I and *Me*	✔	✔				
Pronouns Used as Subject Complements	✔		✔	✔	✔	✔
Pronouns Used as Direct Objects		✔	✔	✔	✔	✔
The Person of Pronouns		✔	✔	✔		
The Gender of Pronouns			✔			
We and *Us*		✔				
Pronouns Used as Objects of Prepositions			✔	✔		

	C	D	E	F	G	H
Pronouns Used in Contractions			✔	✔		
Reflexive Pronouns			✔	✔	✔	
Interrogative Pronouns				✔	✔	✔
Indefinite Pronouns				✔	✔	✔
Double Negatives				✔		
Pronouns Used as Indirect Objects					✔	✔
Who and *Whom*					✔	✔
Pronouns Used after *Than* and *As*					✔	✔
Relative Pronouns					✔	✔
Demonstrative Pronouns					✔	✔
Nothing and *Anything*					✔	
Pronouns Used as Objects of Prepositions						✔
Intensive Pronouns			✔			✔

ADJECTIVES	C	D	E	F	G	H
Descriptive Adjectives	✔			✔	✔	
Adjectives That Tell How Many	✔	✔	✔	✔		
Indefinite and Definite Articles	✔	✔	✔	✔	✔	
Demonstrative Adjectives	✔	✔	✔	✔	✔	✔
Comparative Forms of Adjectives	✔	✔	✔	✔	✔	✔
Possessive Adjectives		✔	✔	✔		
Common and Proper Adjectives		✔	✔			✔
Good and *Bad*		✔				
The Position of Adjectives			✔	✔	✔	✔
Superlative Forms of Adjectives			✔	✔	✔	✔
Adjectives Used as Subject Complements				✔		
Words Used as Adjectives or Nouns				✔	✔	✔
Those and *Them*				✔		
Interrogative Adjectives				✔		
Fewer and *Less*					✔	

ADVERBS	C	D	E	F	G	H
Adverbs of Time	✔	✔	✔	✔		
Adverbs of Place	✔	✔	✔	✔		
Good and *Well*	✔	✔	✔			
Comparative Adverbs		✔	✔	✔		✔
Adverbs of Manner		✔	✔	✔		
No, *Not*, and *Never*		✔	✔	✔		
Superlative Adverbs			✔	✔		
Real and *Very*			✔			
Their and *There*			✔	✔		
To, *Too*, and *Two*			✔	✔		

Adverbs and Adjectives				✔	✔	✔
There, *Their*, and *They're*					✔	
Farther and *Further*					✔	✔
Interrogative Adverbs					✔	✔
Adverbial Nouns					✔	✔
As . . . As, *So . . . As*, and *Equally*						✔

PUNCTUATION, CAPITALIZATION, ABBREVIATIONS	C	D	E	F	G	H
End Punctuation	✔	✔	✔	✔	✔	✔
Periods after Abbreviations, Titles, and Initials	✔	✔				
Capital Letters	✔	✔	✔	✔	✔	
Titles of Books and Poems	✔		✔	✔	✔	
Commas Used in Direct Address	✔	✔	✔	✔		
Punctuation in Direct Quotations	✔	✔	✔	✔		
Apostrophes		✔	✔			
Commas after *Yes* and *No*		✔	✔	✔		
Commas Separating Words in a Series		✔	✔	✔		
Commas after Parts of a Letter			✔	✔		
Commas in Dates and Addresses			✔	✔		
Commas in Geographical Names			✔			
Commas Used with Appositives				✔		
Commas Used in Compound Sentences				✔		
Semicolons and Colons				✔	✔	✔
Apostrophes, Hyphens, and Dashes				✔	✔	✔
Commas and Semicolons						✔

PREPOSITIONS, CONJUNCTIONS, INTERJECTIONS	C	D	E	F	G	H
Prepositions and Prepositional Phrases			✔	✔	✔	✔
Interjections			✔	✔	✔	✔
Between and *Among*			✔	✔		
From and *Off*			✔			
Adjectival Phrases			✔			
Adverbial Phrases			✔			
Coordinate Conjunctions			✔			
Words Used as Prepositions and Adverbs				✔	✔	✔
At and *To*				✔		
Beside and *Besides*, *In* and *Into*				✔		
Coordinate and Correlative Conjunctions					✔	
Conjunctive Adverbs					✔	

	C	D	E	F	G	H
Subordinate Conjunctions					✔	✔
Without and *Unless, Like, As,* and *As If*					✔	✔
PHRASES, CLAUSES	C	D	E	F	G	H
Adjectival Phrases				✔	✔	
Adverbial Phrases				✔	✔	
Adjectival Clauses					✔	✔
Adverbial Clauses					✔	✔
Restrictive and Nonrestrictive Clauses					✔	
Noun Clauses						✔
PARTICIPLES, GERUNDS, INFINITIVES	C	D	E	F	G	H
Participles						✔
Dangling Participles						✔
Gerunds						✔
Infinitives						✔
Hidden and Split Infinitives						✔
WORD STUDY SKILLS	C	D	E	F	G	H
Synonyms	✔	✔	✔	✔		
Antonyms	✔	✔				
Homophones	✔	✔	✔			
Contractions	✔	✔				
Compound Words		✔				
PARAGRAPH SKILLS	C	D	E	F	G	H
Using Colorful Adjectives	✔		✔			
Combining Subjects, Verbs, and Sentences	✔					
Finding the Exact Word		✔				
Using Similes		✔				
Expanding Sentences		✔				
Rewriting Rambling Sentences		✔	✔			
Revising		✔				
Proofreading		✔				
Recognizing the Exact Meaning of Words			✔			
LETTER WRITING	C	D	E	F	G	H
Friendly Letters	✔	✔				
Invitations	✔					
Letters of Acceptance	✔					
Thank-You Letters	✔			✔		
E-Mail Messages	✔	✔		✔		

Envelopes	✔	✔				
Forms	✔	✔				
Business Letters				✔		
RESEARCH	C	D	E	F	G	H
Computer Catalog	✔					
Dictionary	✔	✔				
Encyclopedia	✔		✔			
Thesaurus		✔				
Internet		✔	✔	✔	✔	✔
Almanac			✔			
Atlas			✔		✔	
Guides to Periodicals				✔		
Biographical Information				✔		
The Dewey Decimal System				✔		
Books of Quotations					✔	
Books in Print					✔	
The Statistical Abstract of the United States						✔
Research Tools						✔

Sentence Analysis

Purpose

Sentence analysis is a classroom-tested strategy designed to aid students in the understanding of a sentence through the study of its grammatical components and their relationship to one another.

Sentence analysis begins with a careful and thoughtful reading of the sentence to determine that it does contain a complete thought. Students then determine the *use* of the sentence (for example, declarative). Next, they identify the subject and the predicate. They can then go on to analyze the details in the sentence.

It is often useful to conduct a sentence analysis as an oral exercise. Each student responds to one point in the analysis in some predetermined order—by row, by group, or by number. Keep the responses moving at a fairly fast pace to hold students' interest. Five minutes at the beginning of each grammar period will focus the students on the task. Prolonging the activity may make it a chore rather than a challenge.

Give each student a copy of the Sentence Analysis Chart (page TE16) or place a blown-up version where all students can see it. Select a sentence from this or another book and write it on the board for analysis.

Ideally, you should act as an observer during the activity, allowing students to perform the analysis without assistance. The students' performance will indicate their grasp of grammar and help you identify areas that need review.

Consistent practice in identifying grammatical concepts will ensure that students arrive at an understanding of how the English language is structured and how they can use its patterns to express their own thoughts.

Procedure

Display the Sentence Analysis Chart (page TE16) or distribute a copy to each student. Choose a sentence that contains the aspects of grammar recently taught or reviewed and write it on the board. The first few times you do the activity, you may also want to display or distribute the Sentence Analysis Questions (page TE15) to help students complete the task.

Now have students use the chart to work through the steps of analysis, identifying each part of the sentence.

1. Sentence

Have the sentence read aloud. You may want to have the class read as a whole or ask an individual to read. Students should recognize that a sentence has a subject and a predicate and forms a complete thought.

EXAMPLE SENTENCE: **Yesterday the happy children played drums noisily.**

2. Use

Students should be able to recognize that a sentence is declarative, interrogative, imperative, or exclamatory. In selecting sentences for analysis, vary your choice among the four types.

According to *use*, the example sentence is declarative because it makes a statement.

Note: You may want to have students practice steps 1 and 2 several times before moving on to step 3. Once the students are comfortable identifying sentences, add the following steps one at a time, practicing them in short sessions each day.

3. Predicate

The predicate is the part of a sentence that contains a verb. Because the verb is the focal point of the thought, it should be identified first. The verb expresses action or being.

The verb in the example sentence is *played.*

4. Subject

The verb tells what the subject does or is. The subject can be determined by asking *who* or *what* before the verb.

The subject of the example sentence is *children.*

5. Object/Complement

Sometimes the predicate verb is completed by a direct object or a subject complement. They answer the questions *whom, who,* or *what* after the verb.

The direct object of the example sentece is *drums.*

6. Modifiers

Adverbs modify verbs. Adverbs answer the questions *how, when,* or *where.*

In the example sentence, the adverb *yesterday* tells when the children played, and the adverb *noisily* tells how the children played.

Adjectives modify nouns or pronouns. Adjectives answer the questions *what, what kind, how many,* or *whose.* An article is an adjective that points out a noun.

In the example sentence, the article *the* points out the noun *children,* and the adjective *happy* tells what kind of children.

7. Parts of Speech

To close the activity, ask the students to name the part of speech of each word in the sentence, beginning with the first and moving through the sentence in order.

In the example sentence, *yesterday* is an adverb, *the* is an article, *happy* is an adjective, *children* is a noun, *played* is a verb, *noisily* is an adverb.

Sentence Analysis Questions

1. Sentence
Does the group of words form a complete thought with a subject and a predicate? (If it does, it's a sentence.)

2. Use
Is the sentence *declarative* (makes a statement), *interrogative* (asks a question), *imperative* (gives a command), or *exclamatory* (shows surprise or emotion)?

3. Predicate
The predicate of a sentence contains a *verb*. A verb shows action or being. What is the verb in the sentence? (The verb includes the main verb and any helping verbs: *swam/had swum, goes/is going.*)

4. Subject
The *subject* is a noun or a pronoun. The verb tells what the subject does or is. To find the subject, ask *who* or *what* before the verb.

5. Object/Complement
The direct object or subject complement complete the verb. To find them ask *whom, who,* or *what* after the verb.

6. Modifiers
Adverbs tell more about verbs. To find the adverbs, ask *how, when,* or *where* the action or being took place.

Adjectives describe nouns or pronouns. To find the adjectives, ask *what, what kind, how many,* or *whose* about each noun or pronoun. An article is an adjective that points out a noun.

7. Parts of Speech
- Which words name persons, places, or things? (Those words are *nouns.*)
- Which words take the place of nouns? (Those words are *pronouns.*)
- Which words express action or being? (Those words are *verbs.*)
- Which words tell more about verbs? (Those words are *adverbs.*)
- Which words describe nouns? (Those words are *adjectives.*)

Sentence Analysis Chart

Sentence

Use

Predicate

Subject

Object/Complement

Modifiers

Parts of Speech

EXERCISES IN ENGLISH

★ GRAMMAR FOR LIFE ★

LEVEL E

LOYOLAPRESS.

CHICAGO

Consultants
Therese Elizabeth Bauer
Martina Anne Erdlen
Anita Patrick Gallagher
Patricia Healey
Irene Kervick
Susan Platt

Linguistics Advisor
Timothy G. Collins
National-Louis University

Series Design: Karen Christoffersen
Cover Design: Vita Jay Schweighart
Cover Art: Jody Lepinot/prairiestudio.com
Cover Photoshop: Becca Taylor Gay
Interior Art: Stacy Previn/munrocampagna.com
Character Education Portraits: Jim Mitchell
Back Cover Text: Ted Naron

Acknowledgments

page 151   From *The World Almanac and Book of Facts 2000,* © 2001.
                  World Almanac Education Group. All rights reserved.
                  Reprinted by permission.

0-8294-2018-5 ★

0-8294-1745-1 ★

Exercises in English® is a registered trademark of Loyola Press.

Manufactured in the United States of America.

03 04 05 06 07 08 QuebD ★ 10 9 8 7 6 5 4 3 2

03 04 05 06 07 08 QuebD ★ 10 9 8 7 6 5 4 3 2 1

Table of Contents

REVIEW

1 Identifying Sentences   1
Crazy Horse

2 Identifying Declarative and Interrogative Sentences   2

3 Forming Declarative and Interrogative Sentences   3

4 Identifying Imperative and Exclamatory Sentences   4

5 Identifying the Four Kinds of Sentences   5

6 Identifying Subjects and Predicates   6

7 Reviewing Sentences   7–8

NOUNS

8 Identifying Nouns   9

9 Identifying Proper and Common Nouns   10

10 Writing Proper and Common Nouns   11

11 Identifying Singular and Plural Nouns   12

12 Spelling Singular and Plural Nouns   13

13 Identifying the Possessive Forms of Nouns   14

14 Using the Possessive Forms of Nouns   15

15 Using Nouns as Subjects   16

16 Using Subject Complements   17

17 Using Nouns in Direct Address   18

18 Using Nouns as Direct Objects   19

19 Recognizing Direct Objects and Subject Complements   20

20 Using Nouns as Objects of Prepositions   21

21 Recognizing the Uses of Nouns   22
Susan B. Anthony

22 Reviewing Nouns   23–24

PRONOUNS

23 Identifying Singular and Plural Personal Pronouns   25

24 Identifying the Person of a Personal Pronoun   26

25 Recognizing the Person and Gender of a Personal Pronoun   27

26 Using Pronouns as Subjects   28
Mathew Brady

27 Recognizing Pronouns Used as Subject Complements   29

28 Using Pronouns as Subject Complements   30

29 Using Pronouns as Direct Objects   31

30 Using Pronouns as Objects of Prepositions   32

31 Using Subject and Object Pronouns   33

32 Using Subject and Object Pronouns   34

33 Reviewing Subject and Object Pronouns   35

34 Identifying Possessive Pronouns   36

35 Pronouns in Contractions   37

36 Using Reflexive and Intensive Pronouns   38

37 Reviewing Pronouns   39–40

ADJECTIVES

38 Identifying Adjectives   41

39 Forming Proper Adjectives   42

40 Identifying Indefinite and Definite Articles   43
Father Damien

41 Identifying Demonstrative Adjectives   44

42 Using Possessive Adjectives   45

43 Using Adjectives That Tell How Many   46

44 Recognizing the Position of Adjectives   47

45 Forming the Comparative and Superlative Forms of Adjectives   48

46 Reviewing Adjectives   49–50

Verbs

47 Recognizing Action Verbs   51

48 Using Action Verbs   52

49 Writing Action Verbs   53

50 Identifying Verbs of Being   54

51 Recognizing Verbs and Sentences   55

52 Recognizing Verb Phrases   56

53 Recognizing Verb Phrases in Questions and Negative Statements   57

54 Identifying Regular and Irregular Verbs   58

55 Recognizing Regular and Irregular Verbs   59

56 Writing Regular and Irregular Verbs   60

57 Using Forms of *Break* and *See*   61

58 Using Forms of *Go* and *Choose*   62

59 Using Forms of *Take*   63

60 Using Verb Tenses   64

61 Recognizing Simple Verb Tenses   65
Dorothea Dix

62 Recognizing Progressive Verb Tenses   66

63 Recognizing Transitive Verbs   67

64 Recognizing Intransitive Verbs   68

65 Identifying Transitive and Intransitive Verbs   69

66 Using Linking Verbs   70

67 Understanding the Agreement of Subject and Verb   71

68 Using *Is, Are,* and *Am*   72

69 Using *Was* and *Were*   73

70 Using *Does, Doesn't* and *Do, Don't*   74

71 Using Forms of *Let* and *Leave*   75

72 Using Forms of *Lie* and *Lay*   76

73 Using Forms of *Sit* and *Set*   77

74 Using Forms of *Teach* and *Learn*   78

75 Reviewing Verbs   79–80

Adverbs

76 Using Adverbs of Time   81

77 Using Adverbs of Place   82

78 Using Adverbs of Manner   83

79 Reviewing Adverbs of Time, Place, and Manner   84
Father Edward J. Flanagan

80 Comparing with Adverbs   85

81 Using *Good* and *Well*   86

82 Using *Their* and *There*   87

83 Using *Real* and *Very*   88

84 Using *To, Too,* and *Two*   89

85 Using *No, Not,* and *Never*   90

86 Reviewing Adverbs   91–92

Prepositions, Conjunctions, Interjections

87 Recognizing Prepositions and Prepositional Phrases   93

88 Writing Prepositions   94

89 Using *Between* and *Among*   95

90 Using *From* and *Off*   96

91 Recognizing Adjectival Phrases   97

92 Writing Adjectival Phrases   98

93 Recognizing Adverbial Phrases   99

94 Writing Adverbial Phrases   100

95 Distinguishing Between Adjectival and Adverbial Phrases   101
Emma Lazarus

96 Using Conjunctions to Connect Subjects   102

97 Using Conjunctions to Connect Predicates   103

98 Using Conjunctions to Connect Direct Objects   104

99 Using Conjunctions to Connect Sentences   105

100 Using Interjections   106

101 Reviewing Prepositions, Conjunctions, and Interjections   107–108

SENTENCES

102 Reviewing Parts of Speech   109

103 Identifying Subjects and Predicates   110
Norman Rockwell

104 Identifying the Complete Subject   111

105 Identifying the Complete Predicate   112

106 Recognizing Complete Sentences   113

107 Forming Compound Subjects   114

108 Forming Compound Predicates   115

109 Forming Compound Objects   116

110 Reviewing Compound Elements in a Sentence   117

111 Recognizing Natural and Inverted Order in Sentences   118

112 Reviewing the Four Kinds of Sentences   119

113 Writing Different Kinds of Sentences   120

114 Reviewing Sentences   121–122

PUNCTUATION & CAPITALIZATION

115 Using Periods   123

116 Using Commas in a Series and in Parts of a Letter   124

117 Using Commas with Dates and Geographical Names   125

118 Using Commas with Yes and No and with Words in Direct Address   126

119 Using Commas with Quotation Marks   127

120 Using Commas with Conjunctions   128

121 Reviewing Commas   129
Madam C. J. Walker

122 Using Exclamation Points, Question Marks, and Apostrophes   130

123 Using Punctuation in Direct Quotations   131

124 Using Punctuation in Divided Quotations   132

125 Quotation Marks and Underlining in Titles   133

126 Using Capital Letters   134

127 Reviewing Punctuation and Capitalization   135–136

REVISING A PARAGRAPH

128 Using Homophones   137

129 Recognizing Antonyms   138

130 Identifying Synonyms   139

131 Recognizing the Exact Meaning of Words   140

132 Using Action Verbs   141

133 Using Colorful Adjectives   142

134 Rewriting Rambling Sentences   143–144
Kit Carson

135 Letter Writing   145

136 Letter Writing   146

RESEARCH SKILLS

137 Using the Internet: Surfing the Web   147–148

138 Using an Encyclopedia: Main Ideas and Details   149–150

139 Using an Almanac   151–152

140 Using an Atlas: Physical and Political Maps   153–154

SENTENCE DIAGRAMS   155–158

HANDBOOK OF TERMS   159–169

Name _____

1. Identifying Sentences

A **sentence** is a group of words that expresses a complete thought.
A sentence has a subject and a predicate. The subject is who or
what the sentence is about. The predicate tells about the subject.

SUBJECT	PREDICATE
Crazy Horse	was a legendary warrior.
He and Sitting Bull	joined forces at the battle of Little Big Horn.

A. Read each example. Write **S** on the line if the words form a sentence.
Put a period at the end of each sentence.

___[S]___ 1. Crazy Horse was born in what is
            now South Dakota [.]

_____ 2. Son of an Oglala medicine man

___[S]___ 3. His childhood name was Curly [.]

___[S]___ 4. When he was 11, he killed a buffalo [.]

_____ 5. Received a horse as a reward

B. Read each sentence. Draw a line
between the subject and the predicate.

1. Crazy Horse | earned a reputation for skill and daring.

2. His people's traditional way of life | was important to him.

3. The War Department | ordered Crazy Horse's people to reservations.

4. Crazy Horse and his companions | became members of the resistance.

5. Oglala, Cheyenne, and Hunkpapa warriors | banded together.

6. Crazy Horse and Sitting Bull | attacked the cavalry troops.

7. Chief Gall | led the Hunkpapa warriors from the other direction.

8. General Custer's Seventh Cavalry | was destroyed on June 25, 1876.

9. Crazy Horse and his starving people | surrendered on May 6, 1877.

10. He | was stabbed by a soldier and died on September 5.

**Crazy Horse fought for what he believed.
Give an example of how you can stand up for what you believe.**

1

2. Identifying Declarative and Interrogative Sentences

> A **declarative sentence** makes a statement.
> A declarative sentence ends with a period.
>
> **The sun is the largest star in our solar system.**
>
> An **interrogative sentence** asks a question.
> An interrogative sentence ends with a question mark.
>
> **How big is the sun?**

A. Decide whether each sentence is declarative or interrogative. Write your answer on the line.

____[interrogative]____ 1. What is the solar system?

____[declarative]____ 2. The solar system includes the sun and the planets.

____[declarative]____ 3. The sun is a medium-sized star.

____[interrogative]____ 4. Is the sun made of oxygen?

____[interrogative]____ 5. Does the sun go around the earth?

____[declarative]____ 6. The sun is made of hydrogen and helium.

____[declarative]____ 7. The planets revolve around the sun.

____[declarative]____ 8. The moon revolves around the earth.

____[interrogative]____ 9. Why do the planets stay in their orbits?

____[declarative]____ 10. They are held by the sun's gravitational pull.

B. Decide whether each sentence is declarative or interrogative. Write your answer on the line. Add the correct end punctuation.

____[declarative]____ 1. Comets and asteroids orbit the sun [.]

____[interrogative]____ 2. How big can a comet be [?]

____[declarative]____ 3. The tail of a comet can be 186 million miles long [.]

____[interrogative]____ 4. Do you know what asteroids are made of [?]

____[declarative]____ 5. Asteroids are pieces of rock and metal [.]

3. Forming Declarative and Interrogative Sentences

A sentence has a subject and a predicate.

SUBJECT
People in the United States

PREDICATE
have many different kinds of jobs.

An information question can begin with *who, what, where,* or *when.*

A. Choose the best predicate for each subject. Write the letter on the line.
Use each letter once.

1. Factory workers ___[e]___

2. Dairy farmers ___[c]___

3. Cattle ranchers ___[b]___

4. Many people near the ocean ___[a]___

5. People in the city ___[d]___

a. become fishermen.

b. raise cows for meat and leather.

c. provide milk, butter, and cheese.

d. can work in offices or stores.

e. build cars and other machines.

B. Rewrite each sentence as an information question.
Use the question word given.

1. Karen got her first job when she was eleven years old.

   When ___[did Karen get her first job]_____?

2. Her neighbor paid her to pull weeds in his garden.

   Who ___[paid her to pull weeds in his garden]_____?

3. When Karen was in high school, she worked in a drugstore.

   Where ___[did Karen work when she was in high school]_____?

4. In college Karen learned about our polluted oceans.

   Where ___[did Karen learn about our polluted oceans]_____?

5. Now she is studying to become an oceanographer.

   What ___[is she studying now]_____?

4. Identifying Imperative and Exclamatory Sentences

An **imperative sentence** gives a command or makes a request.
An imperative sentence ends with a period.

Do experiments to learn about the water cycle.

An **exclamatory sentence** expresses strong emotion.
An exclamatory sentence ends with an exclamation point.

That is really interesting!

A. Underline the sentences that are imperative.

1. <u>Fill a kettle with water.</u>

2. <u>Put the kettle on the burner.</u>

3. Soon you'll see steam rising from the spout.

4. Watch out!

5. The steam is very hot!

B. Decide whether each sentence is imperative or exclamatory.
Write your answer on the line. Add the correct end punctuation.

_____[imperative]_____ 1. Place an ice cube on a dish [.]

_____[imperative]_____ 2. Set the dish in a sunny area [.]

_____[imperative]_____ 3. Record the time and date [.]

_____[imperative]_____ 4. Watch the ice cube melt [.]

_____[imperative]_____ 5. Write the time the ice melts completely [.]

_____[exclamatory]_____ 6. Be careful [!]

_____[exclamatory]_____ 7. Don't spill the water [!]

_____[imperative]_____ 8. Now watch the water evaporate [.]

_____[imperative]_____ 9. Write the time the water evaporates completely [.]

_____[exclamatory]_____ 10. Isn't that amazing [!]

Name_____

5. Identifying the Four Kinds of Sentences

> A sentence can be declarative, interrogative, imperative, or exclamatory.

A. Put the correct punctuation mark at the end of each sentence.

1. In 1803 Congress purchased the Louisiana Territory from France [.]

2. Meriwether Lewis was President Thomas Jefferson's secretary [.]

3. Jefferson asked Lewis to explore the territory [.]

4. Did Lewis go on the expedition alone [?]

5. He and William Clark led the Corps of Discovery [.]

6. They found a route from the Mississippi River to the Pacific Ocean [.]

7. How far did they go [?]

8. The trip to the Pacific and back covered about 8,000 miles [.]

9. Now, that is an impressive trip [!]

10. The expedition took two years [.]

B. Decide whether each sentence is declarative, interrogative, imperative, or exclamatory. Write your answer on the line. Add the correct end punctuation.

_____[declarative]_____ 1. The journey started in May 1804 [.]

_____[interrogative]_____ 2. Did the explorers go on foot [?]

_____[declarative]_____ 3. They traveled up the Missouri River in keelboats [.]

_____[exclamatory]_____ 4. It must have been difficult [!]

_____[declarative]_____ 5. They spent the winter with the Mandan Indians [.]

_____[declarative]_____ 6. They relied on the Indians for their success [.]

_____[declarative]_____ 7. Sacagawea, a Shoshone, was their guide [.]

_____[declarative]_____ 8. Her brother gave them horses and assistance [.]

_____[exclamatory]_____ 9. That was good luck [!]

_____[imperative]_____ 10. Read more about Lewis and Clark [.]

Review

6. Identifying Subjects and Predicates

A sentence has a subject and a predicate. The **subject** is who or what the sentence is about. The **predicate** tells about the subject.

SUBJECT	PREDICATE
The Revolutionary War	**freed the colonies from the British.**
George Washington	**was the leader of the army.**

A. Underline the complete subject of each sentence.

1. <u>The American Army</u> lost several battles in 1777.
2. <u>General Washington and the army</u> went into winter quarters.
3. <u>The soldiers</u> stayed in Valley Forge, Pennsylvania.
4. <u>The winter of 1777</u> was very cold and snowy.
5. <u>The soldier's clothes</u> were thin and ragged.
6. <u>Almost everyone</u> was hungry and tired.
7. <u>Some of the soldiers</u> got very sick.
8. <u>Others</u> went home to their farms.
9. <u>The government</u> sent food and clothing at last.
10. <u>Washington and his men</u> were ready to fight again.

B. Choose the best word to complete the predicate of each sentence. Write the word on the line. Use each word once.

became	boarded	carried	dressed up	dumped
painted	passed	sailed	stuck	tore

1. In 1773 some English ships ____[sailed]____ into Boston Harbor.

2. The ships ____[carried]____ English tea.

3. The English Parliament had ____[passed]____ a tax on tea.

4. One night some colonists ____[dressed up]____ like Mohawk Indians.

5. They ____[stuck]____ feathers in their hair.

6. They ____[painted]____ their faces with dark colors.

7. The colonists ____[boarded]____ the English ships.

8. They ____[tore]____ open chests of tea.

9. They ____[dumped]____ the tea into the ocean.

10. The Boston Tea Party ____[became]____ famous throughout the colonies.

Name_____

7. Reviewing Sentences

A. Read each example. Write **S** if the words form a sentence.
Put a period at the end of each sentence.

___[S]___ 1. Everyone feels stress sometime [.]

___[S]___ 2. Stress can be good or bad [.]

_____ 3. Worried, afraid, excited, or happy

___[S]___ 4. Too much stress can be bad for your health [.]

_____ 5. Harder to fight sickness

B. Read each sentence. Draw a line between the
subject and the predicate.

1. Any strong emotion | can cause stress.
2. The emotion | might be pleasant or unpleasant.
3. Great excitement | often causes stress.
4. Runners and other athletes | feel stress during a race or game.
5. Stress | can make your mouth feel dry.
6. Your heart | might beat faster.
7. You | might feel tired or nervous.
8. Perspiration | may appear on your skin.
9. Digestion of food | may speed up or slow down.
10. Many health problems | can be blamed on stress.

C. Decide whether each sentence is declarative, interrogative,
imperative, or exclamatory. Write your answer on the line.
Put the correct punctuation mark at the end of each sentence.

____[declarative]____ 1. The changes people experience in life
can cause stress [.]

____[interrogative]____ 2. What can you do to control stress [?]

____[declarative]____ 3. One way to deal with stress is to relax [.]

7

Name_____

_____[imperative]_____ 4. Sit or lie in a comfortable position [.]

_____[imperative]_____ 5. Breathe in deeply while you count to four [.]

_____[imperative]_____ 6. Breathe out slowly while you count to eight [.]

_____[interrogative]_____ 7. Do you feel better [?]

_____[interrogative]_____ 8. Did you know that laughing can cut down on stress [?]

_____[declarative]_____ 9. Smiling makes people feel better [.]

_____[exclamatory]_____ 10. That's great advice [!]

Try It Yourself
Write four sentences about how you deal with stress.
Be sure each sentence is complete.
Use correct punctuation.

_____

_____

_____

_____

Check Your Own Work
Choose a piece of writing from your portfolio or journal,
a work in progress, an assignment from another class,
or a letter. Revise it, applying the skills you have
reviewed. The checklist will help you.

✔ Does each sentence express a complete thought?

✔ Does each sentence start with a capital letter?

✔ Does each sentence end with the correct punctuation mark?

Name _____

8. Identifying Nouns

> A **noun** is a name word. A noun names a person, a place, or a thing.
>
> hiker   campground   tent

A. The following words are nouns. Write each in the proper column.

	PERSON	PLACE	THING
1. uncles	[uncles]		
2. Toledo		[Toledo]	
3. keys			[keys]
4. dashboard			[dashboard]
5. children	[children]		
6. Walbridge Park		[Walbridge Park]	
7. William	[William]		
8. streetlight			[streetlight]
9. Cleveland		[Cleveland]	
10. automobile			[automobile]

B. Underline the nouns in each sentence. The number of nouns in each sentence is in parentheses.

1. <u>Mildred Taylor</u> wrote a <u>book</u> called *The Gold Cadillac*. (3)

2. The <u>father</u> in the <u>story</u> bought an expensive <u>car</u>. (3)

3. His <u>wife</u> had wanted to save <u>money</u> for a <u>house</u>. (3)

4. The <u>father</u> and the <u>children</u> drove to <u>Detroit</u> to visit <u>relatives</u>. (4)

5. The <u>mother</u> refused to go and decided to stay at <u>home</u>. (2)

C. Complete each sentence with nouns. [Answers will vary.]

1. The next trip was to _____ and _____.

2. They stopped at a _____ and a _____.

3. The family spoke to a _____ and _____.

4. They stayed at a _____ and _____.

5. The children brought home a _____ and a _____.

Nouns

9

9. Identifying Proper and Common Nouns

> There are two main kinds of nouns: proper nouns and common nouns.
> A **proper noun** names a particular person, place, or thing.
>
> **Queen Elizabeth**   **London**   **Westminster Abbey**
>
> A **common noun** names any one member of a group of persons, places, or things.
>
> **queen**   **city**   **church**

Nouns

A. Underline each proper noun. Circle each common noun.

1. <u>Japan</u> gave the <u>United States</u> some cherry (trees).

2. These (trees) were planted around the <u>Tidal Basin</u> in <u>Washington, D.C.</u>

3. Beautiful (flowers) bloom on these (trees) in <u>April</u>.

4. The (blossoms) are pink and white.

5. The (flowers) last for only ten or twelve (days).

6. (Photographers) from many (countries) take (pictures) of the (flowers).

7. The <u>Jefferson Memorial</u> is also decorated by these beautiful (flowers).

8. In <u>Japan</u> the (people) have a (festival) when the first (buds) appear.

9. <u>Washington, D.C.,</u> holds a <u>Cherry Blossom Festival</u>.

10. The <u>United States</u> has received a beautiful (gift) from the (people) of <u>Japan</u>.

B. Complete each sentence with a proper noun to match the common noun.

1. My Uncle Mike bought a new _____**[Answers will vary.]**_____.
   car

2. Jessica shopped at _____ for the gift.
   store

3. We went to _____ for our vacation.
   place

4. After the game _____ treated us to a hamburger.
   person

5. Carlos read _____ for one hour.
   book

10. Writing Proper and Common Nouns

A. Write a common noun for each proper noun. **[Answers will vary. Samples are given.]**

		COMMON NOUN			COMMON NOUN
1.	Canada	[country]	11.	Boston	[city]
2.	Brian	[boy]	12.	Easter	[holy day]
3.	Florida	[state]	13.	Sunday	[day]
4.	March	[month]	14.	Alps	[mountains]
5.	Donald Duck	[cartoon]	15.	Pacific Ocean	[ocean]
6.	North America	[continent]	16.	Abraham Lincoln	[president]
7.	Thanksgiving	[holiday]	17.	Memorial Day	[holiday]
8.	Superdome	[stadium]	18.	Alexander Bell	[inventor]
9.	Brown University	[school]	19.	Buick	[car]
10.	Burger Bin	[restaurant]	20.	Mississippi River	[river]

B. Write a proper noun suggested by each common noun. **[Answers will vary.]**

		PROPER NOUN			PROPER NOUN
1.	man	_____	11.	mountains	_____
2.	country	_____	12.	ocean	_____
3.	singer	_____	13.	statue	_____
4.	president	_____	14.	general	_____
5.	astronaut	_____	15.	car	_____
6.	holiday	_____	16.	inventor	_____
7.	comic strip	_____	17.	street	_____
8.	lake	_____	18.	store	_____
9.	detective	_____	19.	movie star	_____
10.	game	_____	20.	restaurant	_____

C. Complete the sentences with proper nouns. **[Answers will vary.]**

In _____ my family visited _____ during the _____
      1. month   2. place   3. holiday

weekend. My friend _____ came with us. I saw _____ for the
               4. person   5. thing

first time.

11. Identifying Singular and Plural Nouns

> A **singular noun** names one person, place, or thing.
> A **plural noun** names more than one person, place, or thing.
>
> | SINGULAR | PLURAL |
> |----------|--------|
> | nut | nuts |
> | cracker | crackers |

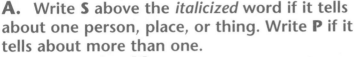

A. Write **S** above the *italicized* word if it tells about one person, place, or thing. Write **P** if it tells about more than one.

1. The potato *chip* [S] is an American *creation* [S].
2. The chips were introduced in a New York health *spa* [S].
3. *Guests* [P] at the spa had eaten thin potato *fries* [P] in France.
4. A *chef* [S] at the spa tried to copy the thin French *fries* [P].
5. The *cook* [S] cut the *potatoes* [P] too thin for fries.
6. These too-thin fried potatoes cooled and were called Saratoga *chips* [P].
7. *People* [P] liked the *mistake* [S] and frequently nibbled this salty *snack* [S].
8. The *chef* [S] was a Native American *chief* [S] named George Crum.
9. Today *Americans* [P] eat about 600 million *pounds* [P] of chips per *year* [S].
10. The *recipe* [S] is so famous that it is in the White House *cookbook* [S].

B. Complete each sentence with the plural *(pl.)* or the singular *(s.)* of the noun.

Pretzel *(pl.)*   1. __[Pretzels]__ were first baked by an Italian monk.

prayer *(pl.)*   2. Monks gave pretzels to children for learning their __[prayers]__.

roll *(pl.)*   3. They took long thin __[rolls]__ of dough and folded them up.

arm *(pl.)*   4. The folds looked like the __[arms]__ of children at prayer.

year *(pl.)*   5. For many __[years]__ the dough was baked soft like bread.

bakers *(s.)*   6. A young __[baker]__ fell asleep while he was making pretzels, and they got very hard.

Customer *(pl.)*   7. __[Customers]__ liked the hard, crunchy pretzels.

Shopkeeper *(pl.)*   8. __[Shopkeepers]__ discovered that hard pretzels stayed fresh longer than soft pretzels.

treat *(pl.)*   9. These __[treats]__ can be made in your own kitchen.

factories *(s.)*   10. Julius Sturgis, a Pennsylvanian, opened the first pretzel __[factory]__.

12. Spelling Singular and Plural Nouns

The plural of most nouns is formed by adding -s or -es to the singular. The plural of nouns ending in *y* after a vowel is formed by adding -s to the singular form. The plural of nouns ending in *y* after a consonant is formed by changing the *y* to *i* and adding -es.

cow	cows	fox	foxes	bunny	bunnies	key	keys
apple	apples	radish	radishes	berry	berries	boy	boys

The plural of some nouns is irregular.

wolf	wolves	goose	geese	ox	oxen	sheep	sheep
wife	wives	man	men	child	children	corn	corn

Read the letter and form plurals where needed.

Dear Mom and Dad,

I love visiting Uncle Ted on his farm. One day

we picked ___[peaches]___ and ___[cherries]___. At first, I wasn't
       1. peach   2. cherry

a good picker. Uncle Ted told me that the small field

___[mice]___ would eat all the fruit that I dropped.
3. mouse

The cherries were so fresh that we didn't need ___[knives]___ to get the ___[leaves]___ off.
                                4. knife   5. leaf

Sometimes we only had to shake the ___[branches]___. The fruit was then packed in
                                     6. branch

___[boxes]___ to be shipped to many ___[factories]___, where it will be made into _____.
7. box   8. factory   9. jelly

We will have to look for the ___[jars]___ at the supermarket.
                          10. jar

Later in the week Ned and I paddled a _____ on the lake. It was so quiet
                                      11. canoe

that I saw many _____ with their ___[babies]___. I thought that I would see only
                12. deer   13. baby

___[herds]___ of sheep and ___[cows]___. This is a great vacation.
14. herd   15. cow

                                         Your son,
                                         Joey

13. Identifying the Possessive Forms of Nouns

The **possessive form** of a noun expresses possession or ownership. The apostrophe (') is the sign of a possessive noun. To form the possessive of a singular noun, add 's to the singular form.

> architect   architect's

To form the possessive of a plural noun that ends in s, add an apostrophe (') to the plural form.

> farmers   farmers'

To form the possessive of a plural noun that does not end in s, add 's to the plural form.

> children   children's

A. Rewrite the following using singular possessive nouns.

1. the whistle of the referee   [the referee's whistle]

2. the voice of the coach   [the coach's voice]

3. the horse of Paul Revere   [Paul Revere's horse]

4. the badge of the officer   [the officer's badge]

5. the spurs of the cowboy   [the cowboy's spurs]

B. Rewrite the following using plural possessive nouns.

1. the cries of the babies   [the babies' cries]

2. the suggestions of both men   [both men's suggestions]

3. the wishbones of the turkeys   [the turkeys' wishbones]

4. the carts of the golfers   [the golfers' carts]

5. the tractors of the farmers   [the farmers' tractors]

C. Underline the correct possessive form of the noun in each sentence.

1. The circus (ringmaster's ringmasters') voice announced the next act.

2. A (lion's lions') roar caused excitement.

3. All of the (elephant's elephants') tails had pink bows on them.

4. All of the (child's children's) eyes followed the tightrope walker.

5. One (acrobat's acrobats') trick amazed everyone.

Name_____

14. Using the Possessive Forms of Nouns

> A noun has a singular and a plural possessive form.

A. Write the singular possessive and the plural possessive of each noun.

	SINGULAR POSSESSIVE	PLURAL POSSESSIVE
1. doctor	[doctor's]	[doctors']
2. baby	[baby's]	[babies']
3. wolf	[wolf's]	[wolves']
4. child	[child's]	[children's]
5. fox	[fox's]	[foxes']

B. Complete each sentence with the correct possessive form of the noun. Use a capital letter when necessary.

national parks   1. Grizzly bears are one of the [national parks'] protected species.

Alaska   2. One of [Alaska's] claims to fame is the grizzly, a type of brown bear.

grizzlies   3. [Grizzlies'] bodies are massive, sometimes being eight feet long and weighing as much as 900 pounds.

cubs   4. A grizzly's den may contain its cubs and the [cubs'] food.

bear   5. This [bear's] claws are straight and not good for climbing.

camper   6. Every [camper's] fear is to encounter a grizzly.

food   7. [Food's] presence at a campsite can attract a bear.

human   8. A [human's] response to seeing a grizzly can range from excitement to terror.

nature   9. Another of [nature's] wild creatures is the puma.

puma   10. The [puma's] many other names include catamount, panther, and mountain lion.

jungle   11. The puma is among the [jungle's] inhabitants, but it is also found in mountains and deserts.

kittens   12. Its [kittens'] behavior is very playful.

cat   13. A domestic [cat's] instincts are similar to a puma's.

deer   14. Many [deer's] lives have been cut short by hungry pumas.

hunters   15. [Hunters'] means of catching pumas are traps and open pits.

15. Using Nouns as Subjects

A sentence has a subject and a predicate. The simple subject is usually the noun that names the person, place, or thing the sentence is about.

The brave <u>firefighters</u> rushed into the burning building.

A. Underline the simple subject in each sentence.

1. Many <u>tribes</u> lived along the Atlantic coastline.
2. These <u>Native Americans</u> lived there long before the arrival of Columbus.
3. <u>Villages</u> were located near lakes and rivers.
4. Six large <u>tribes</u> lived in the area from Canada to Florida.
5. A <u>tribe</u> was an independent nation.
6. The <u>leader</u> of a tribe was called a sachem.
7. The <u>sachem</u> inherited the role from his father.
8. A <u>council</u> of village leaders served with the chief.
9. The first <u>colonists</u> were helped by these Native Americans.
10. <u>Chief Massasoit</u> aided the Pilgrims.

B. Complete each sentence with a subject noun. Use each noun only once.

queen	island	Arthur	knights	sword
legend	king	wife	stone	court

1. King Arthur's ___[sword]___ was named Excalibur.
2. A large ___[stone]___ had the sword stuck into it.
3. ___[Arthur]___ alone was able to pull the sword out of the stone.
4. The ___[court]___ of King Arthur was at Camelot.
5. Brave ___[knights]___ like Sir Lancelot would attend the court.
6. The ___[wife]___ of King Arthur was named Guinevere.
7. The ___[queen]___ fell in love with Sir Lancelot.
8. One ___[legend]___ tells about Arthur's sister, Morgan Le Fay.
9. The ___[island]___ of Avalon was ruled by Morgan Le Fay.
10. The ___[king]___ went to his sister's island to be healed of his wounds.

16. Using Subject Complements

> A **subject complement** is a noun, pronoun, or adjective that completes the meaning of a linking verb in a sentence. It renames or describes the subject.
>
> SUBJECT   SUBJECT COMPLEMENT
> **Debbie** is a certified fitness **instructor**.

A. Circle the simple subject in each sentence. Underline the subject complement.

1. (Snoopy) is a black-and-white beagle.
2. (Charlie Brown) is the owner of Snoopy.
3. (Woodstock) is a small yellow bird.
4. (Woodstock) is Snoopy's friend.
5. In the winter (Woodstock) is a hockey player on his frozen birdbath.
6. In the summer the (birdbath) is Woodstock's swimming pool.
7. (Snoopy) is a baseball player too.
8. (Charlie Brown) is the manager of the baseball team.
9. The other (players) are friends of Charlie Brown.
10. (Charles Schulz) was the creator of all these characters.

B. Complete each sentence with a noun used as a subject complement.

1. A famous school is _____ [Answers will vary.] _____.
2. In school my favorite subject is _____.
3. My teacher is _____.
4. The student across from me is _____.
5. In our school the principal is _____.

C. Complete each sentence with the correct subject complement.

   capital   name   **Dairy State**   bird   range

1. Wisconsin is the ____[Dairy State]____.
2. Denver is the _____[capital]_____ of Colorado.
3. Sierra Nevada is a mountain _____[range]_____.
4. Missouri is the _____[name]_____ of a state and a river.
5. The cardinal is the state _____[bird]_____ of Illinois.

17. Using Nouns in Direct Address

> A noun is used in direct address when it names the person spoken to.
> **<u>Doctor</u>, do you think I have pneumonia?**

A. Underline the noun in direct address in each sentence.

1. <u>Folks</u>, step right up and get your tickets.

2. Be careful, <u>boys</u>, going down the steps.

3. These are box seats, <u>Dad</u>!

4. <u>Mr. Martinez</u>, do you think we will be able to get autographs?

5. Maybe, <u>Jim</u>, we might get a few of them.

6. <u>Fans</u>, please stand for the national anthem.

7. Step up to the plate, <u>batter</u>.

8. I don't think that was a strike, <u>Dad</u>!

9. <u>Jim and Todd</u>, do you want hot dogs?

10. Do you want mustard, <u>boys</u>, on the hot dogs?

B. Complete each sentence with a noun in direct address.

Mrs. Velez   Nurse Higgens   Coach   Rosa   Doctor

1. Where does your arm hurt, _____[Rosa]_____?

2. Bring me Rosa's chart, _____[Nurse Higgens]_____.

3. _____[Doctor]_____, is my arm broken?

4. _____[Mrs. Velez]_____, your daughter will be in a cast for six weeks.

5. I won't be able to play in the game on Saturday, _____[Coach]_____.

C. Write sentences using each word as a noun in direct address. Vary the position of the noun. **[Sentences will vary.]**

José	1.	_____
Laura	2.	_____
class	3.	_____
Coach	4.	_____
swimmers	5.	_____

Name_____

18. Using Nouns as Direct Objects

The **direct object** answers the question *whom* or *what* after an action verb in a sentence.

> **After waiting in line for hours, we managed to purchase two <u>tickets</u> for the show.**
> (Tickets answers the question *what—What* did we manage to purchase?)

> **The show stars my favorite <u>singer</u>.**
> (Singer answers the question *whom—Whom* does the show star?)

A. Circle the direct object in each sentence. Write on the line whether it answers the question *whom* or *what.*

[whom] 1. During the American Revolution, Connecticut produced two famous (men).

[whom] 2. Connecticut claims (Nathan Hale) as a hero.

[what] 3. At first Nathan Hale taught (school.)

[what] 4. Washington needed (information) about the British troops.

[what] 5. Hale joined the (army) of George Washington.

[what] 6. In his schoolmaster's clothes Hale crossed the British (lines.)

[what] 7. On the British side Hale drew (maps) of the British locations.

[what] 8. He hid the (maps) and (information) in his shoes.

[whom] 9. Unfortunately, a British soldier recognized (Hale.)

[whom] 10. The British hanged (Nathan Hale) for spying.

B. Complete each sentence with a direct object. Use each noun once.

battles   information   forts   town   marks
traitor   soldier   sides   hero   Benedict Arnold

1. Connecticut also produced a ___[traitor]___.
2. Americans remember ___[Benedict Arnold]___ as a spy.
3. American General Arnold planned ___[battles]___ with courage and skill.
4. This traitor leaked ___[information]___ to the British.
5. Benedict Arnold changed ___[sides]___ during the war.
6. For the British, General Arnold captured two American ___[forts]___.
7. During battle Arnold's troops killed every ___[soldier]___ in one fort.
8. His troops also burned the ___[town]___ of Griswald.
9. After the war Britain accepted its ___[hero]___ as a citizen.
10. Nathan Hale and Benedict Arnold left their ___[marks]___ on history.

19. Recognizing Direct Objects and Subject Complements

Nouns

Read each sentence. Write **DO** on the line if the *italicized* word is a direct object. Write **SC** if it is a subject complement.

_[SC]_ 1. Tropical rain forests are the earth's oldest living *ecosystems*.

_[DO]_ 2. Rain forests cover only a small *part* of the earth's surface.

_[SC]_ 3. They are *home* to half the plant and animal species on the earth.

_[DO]_ 4. Rain falls up to eight *meters* a year.

_[DO]_ 5. Rain forests have no dry or cold *seasons*.

_[DO]_ 6. A tropical rain forest has four *layers*.

_[SC]_ 7. The emergent layer is the highest *layer* in a rain forest.

_[DO]_ 8. The canopy contains the *tops* of the tallest trees.

_[DO]_ 9. The emergent layer and the canopy receive the most *sunshine*.

_[SC]_ 10. Most rain forest animals are *inhabitants* of the top layers.

_[SC]_ 11. The fourth layer of a rain forest is the *understory*.

_[DO]_ 12. Tree roots, soil, and decaying material make up the forest *floor*.

_[DO]_ 13. The understory and the forest floor receive very little *light*.

_[SC]_ 14. Large animals are *residents* of the forest floor.

_[SC]_ 15. Foods such as bananas, chocolate, and pepper are *products* of rain forests.

_[SC]_ 16. These foods are maintainable *resources*.

_[DO]_ 17. The Amazon rain forest covers an *area* about two-thirds the size of the continental United States.

_[SC]_ 18. It is the world's largest *rain forest*.

_[DO]_ 19. Rain forests help control the world's *climate*.

_[DO]_ 20. Rain forests affect *everyone* on Earth.

Name_____

20. Using Nouns as Objects of Prepositions

> **Prepositions** can show place, time, direction, and relationship. Some common prepositions are *in, into, on, to, by, for, from, at, of, with,* and *without.*
> A prepositional phrase consists of a preposition and a noun or pronoun.
> The word that follows the preposition is called the object of the preposition.
> **The group of <u>fans</u> cheered at the <u>appearance</u> of the <u>singer</u>.**

Nouns

A. Underline the prepositions in the sentences. Circle the object of each preposition. Some sentences have more than one prepositional phrase.

1. The bat hangs upside-down <u>in</u> its (cave.)
2. The sharp claws <u>on</u> its (toes) cling <u>to</u> the (ceiling.)
3. Bats sleep <u>in</u> this (position.)
4. <u>At</u> (night) the bat awakes.
5. Its lips push <u>into</u> the (shape) <u>of</u> a (horn.)
6. Squeaking sounds come <u>from</u> its (throat.)
7. The noise vibrates the air <u>in</u> the (cave.)
8. The bat listens <u>for</u> (echoes) <u>from</u> its (squeaks.)
9. <u>From</u> its (squeaks) the bat can "see" anything <u>in</u> the (dark.)
10. Bats are not blind <u>in</u> the (daylight.)

B. Complete the paragraph by adding objects of the prepositions. [Answers will vary.]

   My friends dared me, so I walked into _____. The insides were

covered with _____. But I kept walking. Soon my ears heard sounds

from _____. I felt a chill run down _____. I had a lump in

_____. My feet were stuck to _____. Suddenly I felt a cold

hand on _____. A cry finally came from _____. Turning

around, I saw a man with _____ in _____.

C. Finish the paragraph with one or two sentences.

_____

_____

_____

21

21. Recognizing the Uses of Nouns

Nouns can be used in different ways.

S—subject	The <u>doctor</u> wrote the prescription.
SC—subject complement	She is a <u>surgeon</u>.
DO—direct object	She has a <u>degree</u> from Harvard University.
OP—object of preposition	She practices with several <u>doctors</u>.
DA—direct address	<u>Doctor</u>, do I have a temperature?

Underline each noun. Above each noun write its use.
Use the letters given in the box above.

1. <u>Shelley</u>[DA], did you vote in the <u>election</u>[OP]?

2. Yes, <u>Erica</u>[DA], I cast my <u>ballot</u>[DO].

3. <u>Women</u>[S] didn't always have the <u>right</u>[DO] to vote in <u>America</u>[OP].

4. They gained this <u>right</u>[DO] in <u>1920</u>[OP] through the <u>Nineteenth Amendment</u>[OP].

5. <u>Susan B. Anthony</u>[S] fought for this <u>right</u>[OP].

6. The <u>right</u>[S] to vote is also called <u>suffrage</u>[DO].

7. <u>Anthony</u>[S] was a <u>suffragist</u>[SC].

8. She appeared before <u>Congress</u>[OP] on this <u>matter</u>[OP].

9. She and a <u>friend</u>[S] published a <u>newspaper</u>[DO].

10. The <u>name</u>[S] of their <u>paper</u>[OP] was *The Revolution*[SC].

11. Dress <u>reform</u>[S] for <u>women</u>[OP] was also her <u>cause</u>[SC].

12. She cut her <u>hair</u>[DO] short.

13. She even wore <u>bloomers</u>[DO].

14. Many <u>people</u>[S] did not approve of this <u>attire</u>[OP].

15. <u>Women</u>[S] should thank <u>Susan B. Anthony</u>[DO].

Susan B. Anthony fought for women's causes.
Give an example of how you can help a cause that you believe in.

Nouns

Name_____

22. Reviewing Nouns

A. Write on the line whether the *italicized* noun is a person, a place, or a thing.

___[person]___ 1. The French *people* gave America a gift in 1884.

___[thing]___ 2. This gift was the *Statue of Liberty*.

___[thing]___ 3. This *monument* was a sign of friendship and liberty.

___[person]___ 4. *Édouard de Laboulaye*, a historian, suggested the idea.

___[place]___ 5. The people of *France* donated money for the statue.

B. Write on the line whether the *italicized* noun is common or proper.

___[proper]___ 1. *Frédéric Auguste Bartholdi* designed the statue.

___[common]___ 2. The statue was to be built as a proud *woman*.

___[common]___ 3. Her *crown* was made with seven spikes.

___[common]___ 4. The spikes represented the world's seven seas and *continents*.

___[proper]___ 5. She holds a book with the date of the
Declaration of Independence on it.

C. Write on the line whether the *italicized* noun is the subject,
the direct object, or the object of a preposition.

___[subject]___ 1. The *engineer* of the statue was Alexandre Gustave Eiffel.

___[direct object]___ 2. Eiffel built the *skeleton* for the copper body.

___[object of a preposition]___ 3. Sheets of copper were hammered on the *frame*.

___[subject]___ 4. Bartholdi's *mother* was the model for the face.

___[direct object]___ 5. These two Frenchmen shared their *talents* with America.

D. Circle the subject in each sentence.
Draw a line under the subject complement.

1. The (statue) is a female figure 151 feet tall.

2. The (base) of the statue is a pedestal 154 feet high.

3. The (crown) of the statue is an observation deck.

4. The (lights) in the torch are powerful electric lamps.

5. The (home) for this great lady is New York Harbor.

CONTINUED

E. Circle the noun in direct address in each sentence.

1. (Dad,) do we really own that red convertible?
2. Yes, we sure do, (Danielle.)
3. Would you like to go for a ride, (children)?
4. Do you want to come along, (Mom)?
5. Sure. (Molly) would you get my purse?

F. Write on the line whether the *italicized* noun is a direct object or a subject complement.

_____[subject complement]_____ 1. Our last car was a *sedan*.

_____[direct object]_____ 2. Dad bought the *convertible* from a nearby dealer.

_____[direct object]_____ 3. It has leather *seats*.

_____[subject complement]_____ 4. The car is a beautiful *machine*.

_____[direct object]_____ 5. Dad gave us a wonderful *surprise*.

Try It Yourself

Write four sentences about a place you know. Think about your use of nouns. Check your spelling of proper, plural, and possessive nouns.

_____

_____

_____

_____

Check Your Own Work

Choose a selection from your writing portfolio, your journal, a work in progress, an assignment from another class, or a letter. Revise it, applying the skills you have reviewed. The checklist will help you.

✔ Have you capitalized all proper nouns?

✔ Have you used the correct plural forms?

✔ Have you used the apostrophe correctly?

✔ Have you chosen nouns that create a word picture?

Nouns

Name _____

23. Identifying Singular and Plural Personal Pronouns

A **personal pronoun** takes the place of a noun.

> **The fishermen hauled in the net.**   **Mrs. Murphy teaches school.**
> **They hauled in the net.**   **She teaches school.**

A personal pronoun is singular when it refers to one person, place, or thing.

> **He is a computer whiz.**

A personal pronoun is plural when it refers to more than one person, place, or thing.

> **We were caught in a torrential downpour.**

A. Write **S** on the line if the *italicized* pronoun in each sentence is singular or **P** if it is plural.

__[P]__ 1. Our teacher read *us* a story about Harry S Truman.

__[S]__ 2. *It* was a biography by David R. Collins.

__[S]__ 3. *I* saw the book in the library once.

__[S]__ 4. Mrs. Raul read *it* to us a chapter at a time.

__[S]__ 5. *She* always waited until after recess.

__[P]__ 6. *We* could hardly wait to hear about Harry.

__[S]__ 7. The Bowman twins like the part about *him* on the farm.

__[P]__ 8. *They* lived on a farm too.

__[P]__ 9. The Truman family owned cows; Harry milked *them*.

__[S]__ 10. *He* had other chores to do also.

B. Write a pronoun to take the place of the *italicized* words.

1. *The Truman children* worked hard on the farm.

   __[They]__ worked hard on the farm.

2. Early each morning *Harry* went to the barn.

   Early each morning __[he]__ went to the barn.

3. He walked *the goats* to the public spring.

   He walked __[them]__ to the public spring.

4. Mrs. Truman raised chickens in *a large hen house*.

   Mrs. Truman raised chickens in __[it]__ .

5. Every day *Vivian* gathered eggs from the hens.

   Every day __[she]__ gathered eggs from the hens.

Name_____

24. Identifying the Person of a Personal Pronoun

A personal pronoun names the speaker; the person spoken to; or the person, place, or thing spoken about.

The personal pronouns that name the speaker are *I, me, we,* or *us.* (first person)

> **I** wish the weather would change.   The book was a gift to **me**.
> **We** wish Joe would stop by.   Sue and Harry waited for **us**.

The personal pronoun that names the person spoken to is *you.* (second person)

> **Why don't you borrow my umbrella?**

The personal pronouns that name the person, place, or thing spoken about are *he, she, it, him, her, they,* and *them.* (third person)

> **He** spent all his money.   Give the present to **him**.
> **She** brought the cookies to school.   Sarah would like to meet **her**.
> **They** always make a lot of noise.   Does the policeman believe **them**?

A. Underline the personal pronoun(s) that names the speaker.

1. Thoughtfully, I waited on the stage for the spelling bee to begin.

2. We were all a bit nervous.

3. During the contest my teacher smiled encouragingly at me.

4. The judges gave us time to think.

5. I spelled the word very carefully.

B. Underline the personal pronoun(s) that names the person spoken to.

1. Have you ever been in that position?

2. You should try facing an audience!

3. Looking at them, you can feel everyone is pulling for you.

4. Did you hear the word?

5. Could you spell that word?

C. Underline the personal pronoun(s) that names the person or thing spoken about.

1. Joe was very nervous; he laughed when he spelled his word.

2. The crowd laughed with him.

3. They all missed the same word that Joe missed.

4. Not one of them could spell the word.

5. Joe knew how to spell the word, and he won the contest.

Pronouns

25. Recognizing the Person and Gender of a Personal Pronoun

A pronoun can be in the first, second, or third person.
The third person singular pronoun can be masculine, feminine, or neuter.

He made lunch today. (third person, masculine)
She set the table. (third person, feminine)
It was beautiful. (third person, neuter)

A. Write **1** above the personal pronouns that are in the first person. Write **2** above the pronouns in the second person. Write **3** above the pronouns in the third person.

1. [1] We want to give [3] her a present.

2. [3] She has been sick in the hospital.

3. Maybe [1] we should give [3] her a big helium balloon.

4. [3] They will have some ideas for [1] us at the gift store.

5. [1] We asked [3] him for some advice.

6. [3] He said to give [3] him responsibility for finding the right present.

7. When [2] you saw [3] it, [1] we could tell [2] you were disappointed.

8. [3] It was a bunch of fake purple flowers.

9. [1] I didn't like [3] them at all.

10. [1] We all thought [3] they were gaudy.

11. [2] You decided [3] it was up to [1] me to find something better.

12. But the present would still be from all of [1] us.

13. [1] I picked out a pink chenille robe.

14. My friends agreed [3] she would look pretty in pink.

15. So [1] we gave [3] it to [3] her with a nice card.

B. Write **M** above the personal pronouns that are masculine, **F** above the pronouns that are feminine, and **N** above the pronouns that are neuter.

1. [F] She thanked and hugged [M] him.

2. Then [F] she tried [N] it on.

3. [M] He thought [N] it looked good on [F] her.

4. [F] She was smiling when [M] he left [F] her that day.

5. [M] He was happy that [F] she liked [N] it.

Name_____

26. Using Pronouns as Subjects

A pronoun may be used as the subject of a sentence.
The subject pronouns are *I, you, he, she, it, we,* and *they.*

They laughed until tears were streaming down their faces.

A. Circle the subject pronoun in each sentence.

1. (I) just read a book about Mathew Brady.
2. (You) must have heard of him.
3. (He) was born in Warren County, New York, in 1823.
4. At sixteen, (he) moved to New York City to study painting.
5. (I) was surprised at his young age.
6. Soon (he) started to learn photography.
7. (It) had just been introduced in the United States.
8. In 1849 (he) opened a studio in Washington, D.C.
9. (He) began taking photos of famous people.
10. (They) all liked his wonderful pictures.

B. Change the *italicized* word(s) in each sentence to a subject pronoun.
Write the pronoun on the line. Use a capital letter if necessary.

___[It]___ 1. *The Civil War* began in 1861.

[They] 2. *Brady and a group of photographers* took pictures of the battlefields.

___[He]___ 3. *Brady* shocked the world by exhibiting the photos.

[they] 4. For the first time *ordinary people* saw the horror of war.

___[he]___ 5. Later in his life *Brady* fell on hard times.

___[It]___ 6. *Congress* bought his negatives for $25,000.

[She] 7. *My mother* is a big fan of Brady's pictures.

___[We]___ 8. *My family and I* went to an exhibition of his photographs.

[They] 9. *These pictures* are the best known photographs of the Civil War.

___[It]___ 10. *His work* gives us a visual sense of days gone by.

Mathew Brady was always trying to improve his work. Give an example of how you could improve something in your life (a hobby, a project, a friendship, some schoolwork).

Pronouns

Name_____

27. Recognizing Pronouns Used as Subject Complements

A pronoun can replace a noun used as a subject complement. A subject complement follows a verb of being and refers to the same person or thing as the subject of the sentence.

The winner of the award was John.
The winner of the award was <u>he</u>.

A. Circle the correct pronoun. Rewrite each sentence to show the subject complement as the subject.

1. The creators of the spectacle were (they) them).

   [They were the creators of the spectacle.] _____

2. The actress who got sick was (her (she)).

   [She was the actress who got sick.] _____

3. The understudy who filled in was (she) her).

   [She was the understudy who filled in.] _____

4. The author of the scripts was (him (he)).

   [He was the author of the scripts.] _____

5. The orchestra members were (them (they)).

   [They were the orchestra members.] _____

6. The observers of the events were (we) us).

   [We were the observers of the events.] _____

7. The talented costume designer was (he) him).

   [He was the talented costume designer.] _____

8. The critics who panned the show were (them (they)).

   [They were the critics who panned the show.] _____

9. The ushers for the show were (they) them).

   [They were the ushers for the show.] _____

10. Was the ticket seller (she) her)?

    [Was she the ticket seller?] _____

B. Complete each sentence with a subject pronoun. Vary your choices.

[Possible answers are given.]

1. The confident film director was ___[he]___.

2. Is that cheerful makeup artist ___[she]___?

3. The most talented actors are ___[they]___.

4. The worried producer is ___[you]___.

5. The new camera persons are ___[we]___.

29

28. Using Pronouns as Subject Complements

> A subject complement follows a verb of being and refers to the same person or thing as the subject of a sentence. A subject pronoun can be used as a subject complement.

Pronouns

A. Underline the subject complement(s) in each sentence.
Write on the line a pronoun to take the place of the noun(s).

[he]   1. That boy is <u>Brian</u>.

[he/she]   2. That observer is <u>a recruiter</u> from the Boston Ballet Company.

[she]   3. The dancing teacher in the studio is <u>Ms. Lane</u>.

[they]   4. The advanced dancers were <u>Brian, Linda, and Molly</u>.

[he]   5. The piano player is <u>Victor</u>.

[he]   6. The man observing is <u>Mr. Blanc</u>, a retired dance teacher.

[he]   7. Is that <u>Anthony</u> warming up?

[she]   8. The best dancer is <u>Molly</u>.

[they]   9. The newest dancers were <u>Marie and Caroline</u>.

[she] 10. It was <u>Marie</u> who could do the best pirouettes.

B. Complete each sentence with the pronoun specified.

1. Was that __[she]__? *(third, singular, feminine)*

2. No, it was __[he]__. *(third, singular, masculine)*

3. The farmer was __[she]__. *(third, singular, feminine)*

4. The best farmhands were __[they]__. *(third, plural)*

5. The person on the tractor is __[I]__. *(first, singular)*

6. Who is planting beans? It is __[you]__. *(second, singular)*

7. The keepers of the chickens were __[we]__. *(first, plural)*

8. Was it __[you]__ who fed the pigs? *(second, singular)*

9. Yes, it was __[I]__. *(first, singular)*

10. The farmhand in the overalls is __[he]__. *(third, singular, masculine)*

Name_____

29. Using Pronouns as Direct Objects

> A pronoun may be used as the direct object of a verb.
> The object pronouns are *me, you, him, her, it, us,* and *them.*
>
> **The president chose <u>them</u> to be his cabinet members.**

A. Write on the line an object pronoun to take the place of the *italicized* word(s) in each sentence.

[them]   1. At the Soap Box Derby I saw *motorless cars.*

[it]   2. Two boys built *a small wooden box with wheels.*

[him]   3. Beany helped *Foxy* with the design.

[it]   4. Uncle Frankie examined *the model* daily.

[them]   5. Aunt Dottie encouraged *Foxy and Beany.*

[it]   6. Finally the two friends finished *the project.*

[him]   7. At the race, the officials registered *the driver.*

[them]   8. A foxtail on the back of the car puzzled *the judges.*

[it]   9. During the race the car with the foxtail held *the lead.*

[it]   10. Victoriously *the soap box* crossed the finish line.

B. Complete each sentence with an object pronoun. **[Possible answers are given.]**

1. The audience applauded [them] as they received a grand trophy.

2. They held ___[it]___ high in the air.

3. The reporters wanted [them] to say a few words.

4. Uncle Frankie treated [them] after the race.

5. Foxy thanked [him] for the design.

C. Underline the object pronoun in each sentence.

1. Proudly Foxy carried <u>it</u> home.

2. The neighbors met <u>them</u> there.

3. Aunt Dottie praised <u>them</u> for their work.

4. The family wanted <u>them</u> to pose for more pictures.

5. A strong wind pushed <u>it</u> to fame.

30. Using Pronouns as Objects of Prepositions

> An object pronoun may be used as the object of a preposition.
> **The carefully wrapped present was for <u>her</u>.**

Circle the preposition in each sentence. Write on the line the object pronoun that can take the place of the *italicized* words.

_____[them]_____ 1. Today the spotlight would be (on) *Joe Chapin and his classmates*.

_____[him]_____ 2. The teacher looked approvingly (at) *Joe* dressed so nicely.

_____[him]_____ 3. (For) *Joe Chapin* class picture day was exciting!

_____[them]_____ 4. The photographer gave directions (to) *the students*.

_____[it]_____ 5. Then Mr. Ansel looked (into) *the lens*.

_____[them]_____ 6. Next he glanced (at) *the flowering trees*.

_____[them]_____ 7. The location (near) *the trees* was perfect!

_____[it]_____ 8. The class moved (across) *the lawn*.

_____[them]_____ 9. Again the photographer looked (at) *the boys and girls*.

_____[her]_____ 10. Joe stood (behind) *the shortest girl*.

_____[her]_____ 11. Mr. Ansel motioned (toward) *the last girl*.

_____[it]_____ 12. Then he looked (at) *the sky*.

_____[them]_____ 13. Rain had begun to fall (from) *its clouds*.

_____[them]_____ 14. We crowded (under) *the trees* for protection from the rain.

_____[it]_____ 15. Mr. Ansel placed a plastic sheet (over) *his camera*.

31. Using Subject and Object Pronouns

> *I* and *we* are subject pronouns.
> *Me* and *us* are object pronouns.

A. Complete each sentence with the pronoun *I* or *me*.

1. __[I]__ raked the leaves into a pile.

2. Give __[me]__ the rake.

3. That was __[I]__ in the pile of leaves.

4. __[I]__ put the leaves in garbage bags.

5. __[I]__ have finished the yard work.

6. A little dog chased __[me]__ across the yard.

7. __[I]__ like the sight of colored leaves in the fall.

8. Dad will take __[me]__ to the forest preserve to see the red and gold trees.

9. __[I]__ will find pretty leaves and press them in a book.

10. Will you give __[me]__ a paper bag for my collection of leaves?

B. Complete each sentence with the pronoun *we* or *us*.

1. __[We]__ scattered popcorn for the birds.

2. Joe saved some for __[us]__.

3. Did the squirrels see __[us]__?

4. __[We]__ must be sure they don't get the popcorn before the birds do.

5. What's the matter with __[us]__?

6. It's not up to __[us]__ who gets the food.

7. __[We]__ should let whatever is hungry eat it.

8. Joe, will you give __[us]__ some popcorn now?

9. It is __[we]__ who should not have the popcorn.

10. All the butter and salt on it aren't good for __[us]__.

Name_____

32. Using Subject and Object Pronouns

> *He, she,* and *they* are subject pronouns.
> *Him, her,* and *them* are object pronouns.

Pronouns

A. Cross out the incorrect pronoun in parentheses.

1. (They ~~Them~~) are the men and women working on the car.

2. A wrench hit (him ~~he~~) on his hand.

3. Has (he ~~him~~) found the problem?

4. (She ~~Her~~) has given up trying.

5. All the parts puzzle (~~she~~ her).

6. (She ~~Her~~) would rather work at a newspaper.

7. (He ~~Him~~) is a talented mechanic.

8. Mrs. Kervick will pay (them ~~they~~) for their work.

9. Do you know (~~they~~ them)?

10. (He ~~Him~~) brought his car to another shop.

B. Complete each sentence with the correct pronoun.

he/him	1. Is the youngest baby ____[he]____?
they/them	2. The baby followed ____[them]____ into the next room.
They/Them	3. ____[They]____ played with the baby until dinner.
she/her	4. The cook was ____[she]____.
He/Him	5. ____[He]____ put the food on the table.
He/Him	6. ____[He]____ is the boy nearest to the milk jug.
she/her	7. Nora wants ____[her]____ to eat.
They/Them	8. ____[They]____ planned to see a movie after dinner.
he/him	9. His little brother obeyed ____[him]____.
He/Him	10. ____[He]____ finished everything on his plate.
she/her	11. Erica told ____[her]____ about dessert.
they/them	12. Their mother asked ____[them]____ to do the dishes.
She/Her	13. ____[She]____ cleared the dishes from the table.
He/Him	14. ____[He]____ washed the dishes.
they/them	15. Their father drove ____[them]____ to the movie theatre.

Name_____

33. Reviewing Subject and Object Pronouns

> The subject pronouns are *I, you, he, she, it, we,* and *they.*
> The object pronouns are *me, you, him, her, it, us,* and *them.*

A. Underline each personal pronoun. Write **S** on the line if the pronoun is the subject of a sentence or a subject complement. Write **O** on the line if it is a direct object or the object of a preposition.

1. He called her on the phone. [S] ___   [O] ___
2. She told us. [S] ___   [O] ___
3. We talked to him about the phone call. [S] ___   [O] ___
4. The explanation from him didn't satisfy us. [O] ___   [O] ___
5. Did he want her to come along? [S] ___   [O] ___
6. Ask him to have lunch with me. [O] ___   [O] ___
7. We talked about her over hotdogs and fries. [S] ___   [O] ___
8. He and I talked a lot. [S] ___   [S] ___
9. According to him, she is the nicest girl. [O] ___   [S] ___
10. And what does she think of him? [S] ___   [O] ___

B. Circle the correct personal pronoun for each sentence.

1. (We) Us) own four pets: a dog, a cat, and two mice.
2. The barking dog frightened (me) he).
3. (Me (I) heard the dog barking from two blocks away.
4. The one who really loves cats is (she) her).
5. Too bad (you) us) are allergic to cats.
6. (She) Her) likes to play with the cat.
7. Ted put out food for (them) they).
8. (Them (They)) scurry across the floor.
9. Have (you) us) considered getting a pet?
10. Someday (we) us) may add a rabbit to our pet collection.

34. Identifying Possessive Pronouns

> **Possessive pronouns** show possession or ownership. A possessive pronoun can take the place of a possessive noun or of a possessive adjective and the noun for the thing possessed. The possessive pronouns are *mine, ours, yours, his, hers, its,* and *theirs.*
>
> Cole's skateboard is the blue one.　His is the blue one.
> My skateboard is green.　　　　　　Mine is green.

A. Underline the possessive pronoun in each sentence.

1. Is that calculator yours?

2. Hers is on the desk in the second aisle.

3. Mine is in my backpack.

4. His is not here.

5. Do you think we lost ours?

6. Didn't the teacher say we could use hers?

7. I never lend mine to anyone.

8. Yours is older than Vince's.

9. I think hers is the most expensive.

10. Now I remember where ours is.

B. On the line write a possessive pronoun to replace the *italicized* word(s).

____[his]____ 1. The leather-bound book is *Kennedy's.*

____[theirs]____ 2. I lost my book, but I found *Gwen's and Jessica's.*

____[his]____ 3. My book was an early edition, but *Jeremy's* was a first edition.

____[Hers]____ 4. *Julia's book* is the lost one.

____[Ours]____ 5. *Jane's and my dictionaries* are the thickest and the heaviest.

____[mine]____ 6. Have you asked your teacher about *my books*?

____[Yours]____ 7. *Your books* are on the floor in the closet.

____[hers]____ 8. My atlas is more current than *Vanessa's.*

____[his]____ 9. Do you care if I highlight your book or *David's*?

____[Theirs]____ 10. *Tom's and Jessica's notebooks* are sitting on that table in the corner.

35. Pronouns in Contractions

Personal pronouns can be joined with some verbs to form contractions.
An apostrophe (') replaces the missing letter or letters in a contraction.

I am	I'm	we have	we've
you are	you're	he will	he'll
she is	she's	they would	they'd

A. Change each set of words in parentheses to a contraction.
Write the contraction on the line. Use a capital letter when necessary.

1. (I am) __[I'm]__ reading about Boys' Festival Day in Japan.

2. On that day (they will) __[they'll]__ try to fly a 1,600-pound kite.

3. (It is) __[It's]__ an event everyone is looking forward to.

4. (They will) __[They'll]__ paint a fish on the kite.

5. (I have) __[I've]__ learned that the fish is a symbol of courage.

6. (We are) __[We're]__ going to have a kite-flying day at our school.

7. Mrs. Kelly says (she is) __[she's]__ a great kite flyer.

8. (We will) __[We'll]__ see how high her kite goes.

9. (You are) __[You're]__ going to fly your kite, aren't you?

10. (It will) __[It'll]__ be a lot of fun.

B. Write the contraction for the words in parentheses on the line.

(I have) __[I've]__ got a very strange baseball story. (We are) __[We're]__ playing
        1.   2.

a game, and (I am) __[I'm]__ up to bat. I hit the ball so far (they are) __[they're]__ still
                        3.   4.

talking about it! As I run around third base and head for home my teammates shout,

"(You have) __[You've]__ got to go back to first! You didn't tag that base." If I didn't tag
                        5.

it, (I would) __[I'd]__ be out. I crossed the plate and ran to first. I got there just as the
                    6.

ball came in, and the umpire yelled, "(You are) __[You're]__ safe! You get a single."
                                                          7.

"(That is) __[That's]__ not fair!" shouted my teammates.
              8.

"(It is) __[It's]__ the rule," said the ump.
          9.

My teammates told me, "(You are) __[You're]__ the only person to have a five-base
                                    10.

hit and no runs."

36. Using Reflexive and Intensive Pronouns

A **reflexive pronoun** ends in *-self* or *-selves*.

SINGULAR   **myself**   **yourself**   **himself**   **herself**   **itself**
PLURAL   **ourselves**   **yourselves**   **themselves**

A reflexive pronoun often refers to the subject of the sentence.

    He saw <u>himself</u> in the mirror.

Intensive pronouns also end in *-self* or *-selves*.
Intensive pronouns are used for emphasis.

    He <u>himself</u> baked the birthday cake.

A. Underline the reflexive or intensive pronoun in each sentence.

1. At the school play I saw him <u>myself</u>.
2. Did you audition for the play <u>yourself</u>?
3. I <u>myself</u> have been backstage.
4. The student usher closed the doors <u>himself</u>.
5. The teacher <u>herself</u> arranged the stage lighting.
6. The empty stage <u>itself</u> looks very large and intimidating.
7. The girls amused <u>themselves</u> while waiting for the play to begin.
8. Prepare <u>yourself</u> for a spectacular performance.
9. Suddenly I found <u>myself</u> lost in the action of the play.
10. The hurt actor blamed nobody but <u>himself</u> for the accident.

B. Complete each sentence with a correct reflexive or intensive pronoun.

1. The boys ____[themselves]____ wanted to cut the birthday cake.
2. Tina ____[herself]____ made the cake from scratch.
3. You can all help ____[yourselves]____ to some ice cream.
4. They helped ____[themselves]____ to the cake.
5. The cake ____[itself]____ was covered with pink frosting and flowers.
6. The guests exhausted ____[themselves]____ singing and clapping for the birthday girl.
7. I laughed at ____[myself]____ for being so giddy.
8. We ____[ourselves]____ helped clean up after the party.
9. Mike the Magician ____[himself]____ entertained the guests.
10. What present did you ____[yourself]____ bring, Katy?

Pronouns

Name_____

37. Reviewing Pronouns

A. On the line write **1** if the *italicized* pronoun is the speaker, **2** if it is the person spoken to, or **3** if it is the person spoken about.

__[3]__ 1. Clara Barton said *she* needed wagons for the medical supplies.

__[1]__ 2. "But *we* don't have horses for the wagons," the Secretary of War told her.

__[2]__ 3. *You* can't allow the men to be without these things.

__[3]__ 4. *They* need medical supplies badly.

__[2]__ 5. *You* are a brave woman.

__[1]__ 6. Mr. Stanton, allow *me* to go to the battlefield.

__[1]__ 7. That is the place where *I* am needed most.

__[3]__ 8. The wounded require attention before *they* are moved.

__[3]__ 9. Nursing *them* on the battlefield is necessary.

__[2]__ 10. But *you* could get hurt if fighting were to erupt.

B. Circle the reflexive or intensive pronoun in each sentence.

1. She (herself) was called the Angel of the Battlefield.
2. "Clara, prepare (yourself) for the worst," the officers warned.
3. The men helped (themselves) the best they could.
4. I (myself) could never do what Clara did.
5. The work (itself) was difficult, but Clara was determined.

C. On the line write **S** if the *italicized* pronoun is the subject. Write **SC** if it is the subject complement.

__[SC]__ 1. Our swimming teacher is *she*.

__[S]__ 2. *She* taught my brother Christopher.

__[SC]__ 3. The lifeguard is *he*.

__[S]__ 4. At the pool *he* got his swimming badge.

__[S]__ 5. *He* takes his responsibility seriously.

Pronouns

CONTINUED

Name_____

D. Write the correct pronoun on the line.

I/me   1. One day Mrs. Perez asked __[me]__ to read to the class.

She/Her   2. __[She]__ handed me the book.

We/Us   3. __[We]__ were still on Harry Truman's biography.

He/Him   4. __[He]__ had many responsibilities as a child.

they/them   5. Harry did his best with each of __[them]__.

E. Write on the line a possessive pronoun for the *italicized* words in each sentence.

__[Ours]__ 1. *Our library* has other books on Harry Truman.

__[hers]__ 2. Emily wrote *her book report* on one of those books.

__[his]__ 3. Bill told the teacher he forgot *his report*.

__[mine]__ 4. I did *my report* on a book about James Madison.

__[yours]__ 5. Where is *your report*?

F. Write the contraction on the line.

1. we shall   __[we'll]__   4. he would __[he'd]__

2. you have   __[you've]__   5. they are __[they're]__

3. it will   __[It'll]__

Try It Yourself

Write four sentences about a memorable character you have known or read about. Be sure you use pronouns correctly.

_____

_____

_____

_____

Check Your Own Work

Choose a selection from your writing portfolio, your journal, a work in progress, an assignment from another class, or a letter. Revise it, applying the skills you have reviewed. The checklist will help you.

✔ Do your pronouns reflect the correct number and gender?

✔ Did you use subject, object, and possessive pronouns correctly?

✔ Have you placed an apostrophe in each contraction?

Pronouns

Name _____

38. Identifying Adjectives

Some **adjectives** describe nouns or pronouns. Descriptive adjectives tell what kind. Some adjectives come before nouns.

<u>courageous</u> firefighters   <u>messy</u> bedroom   <u>wonderful</u> aroma

A. Underline the descriptive adjectives in each sentence. The number in parentheses tells how many adjectives are in each sentence.

1. The <u>early</u>, <u>golden</u> sun shone on Sadako. (2)
2. It gave her <u>dark</u> hair <u>brown</u> highlights. (2)
3. She looked up at the <u>clear</u> sky. (1)
4. It was a <u>good</u> sign. (1)
5. Sadako went inside the <u>small</u>, <u>neat</u> house. (2)
6. She saw that her <u>big</u> brother was still asleep. (1)
7. "Get up, <u>lazy</u> one!" she said. (1)
8. The <u>delicious</u> smell of food filled the air. (1)
9. <u>Hot</u> eggs and <u>crunchy</u> bacon awaited them in the kitchen. (2)
10. Sadako's <u>sleepy</u> brother dragged himself out of the <u>comfortable</u> bed. (2)

B. Complete each sentence with an adjective. [Possible answers are given.]

atomic	terrible	warm	crisp	Japanese
delicate	younger	soft	little	plain
awful	fresh	front	Memorial	back

1. (Helpful) Sadako dressed her __[younger]__ brother Eiji.
2. She put the __[warm]__ blankets into the (large) closet.
3. In the kitchen her mother sliced __[fresh]__ radishes.
4. This was __[Memorial]__ Day, August 6.
5. On this (sad) day in 1945, an __[atomic]__ bomb fell on Hiroshima.
6. Each year the __[Japanese]__ people remember those who died.
7. Sadako's father came in from the __[back]__ porch.
8. He called for everyone to gather near the __[little]__ altar.
9. A (small) picture of an (older) woman was nearby in a __[delicate]__ frame.
10. Sadako's grandmother had died on that __[terrible]__ day.

C. In addition to the adjectives that you have written on the lines, there are five other adjectives in the sentences in Part B. Circle them.

Name_____

39. Forming Proper Adjectives

Some descriptive adjectives come from proper nouns and are called **proper adjectives**. Proper adjectives begin with a capital letter.

PROPER NOUN	Mexico	Sweden
PROPER ADJECTIVE	Mexican	Swedish

All other adjectives are called common adjectives.

Adjectives

A. Underline the proper adjective in each sentence.

1. Ancient <u>Olympic</u> games were religious festivals.
2. <u>Roman</u> soldiers changed the festivals to contests.
3. The games disappeared from <u>Western</u> culture for fifteen hundred years.
4. A group of <u>German</u> archaeologists found stadium ruins in 1875.
5. A <u>French</u> educator organized the modern competition.
6. The <u>Greek</u> people hosted the first modern games.
7. The Winter Games have often been hosted by the <u>Canadian</u> nation.
8. Recently the Summer Games were hosted by the <u>Korean</u> nation.
9. The <u>Scandinavian</u> nations have talented athletes in the Winter Games.
10. <u>American</u> athletes make us proud in both the Winter and Summer Games.

B. Complete each sentence with the adjective formed from the proper noun at the left.

America   1. The __[American]__ diver scored a perfect 10.

Poland   2. The __[Polish]__ runner finished the marathon in record time.

Russia   3. Dancing her way to fame, the __[Russian]__ skater performed beautifully.

Cuba   4. The __[Cuban]__ players scored the winning point.

France   5. The __[French]__ cyclists pedaled to the top of the Velodrome.

Italy   6. One of the __[Italian]__ relay runners dropped the baton.

Ireland   7. The __[Irish]__ long-distance runner trained in America.

Egypt   8. In the floor exercise the __[Egyptian]__ gymnast performed to modern music.

China   9. Despite the blinding snowstorm the __[Chinese]__ ski jumper outdistanced everyone.

Canada   10. The __[Canadian]__ basketball team lost by only one point.

40. Identifying Indefinite and Definite Articles

> *A, an,* and *the* are **articles**. *A* and *an* are **indefinite articles**. An indefinite article refers to any one of a class of things. *A* is used before words beginning with a consonant sound. *An* is used before words beginning with a vowel sound.
>
> **She ate a banana.**
> **An elephant eats enormous amounts of food.**
>
> *The* is the **definite article**. It refers to one or more specific things.
>
> **She ate the banana that was in the bowl.**
> **The elephants in Lincoln Park Zoo eat tons of food a day.**

Underline the definite and indefinite articles in the reading.

Father Damien was born in the town of Tremeloo, Belgium, on the third of January, 1840. His name then was Joseph de Vesteur. Joseph went to school at a college in Braine-le-Compte. He decided to become a priest and entered an order called the Fathers of the Sacred Heart of Jesus and Mary. At this time he took the name Damien.

Damien was given the assignment of doing mission work in Hawaii. Damien took on the job with great passion. He worked with the natives of the Hawaiian Islands, and he built a number of chapels with his own hands. He is best known for being a missionary to the lepers in the settlement on the island of Molokai. This work showed great courage, because leprosy is a highly contagious disease. Damien ministered to the lepers, who had no doctors or nurses to care for them. He did this in the ways he could, by helping them build houses, by dressing their sores, by comforting them, even by digging their graves. Father Damien ministered to these sick people until he himself contracted leprosy and died.

Father Damien helped people who had no one else to take care of them. Think of a person who needs care and attention. Give an example of how you can help that person.

41. Identifying Demonstrative Adjectives

The **demonstrative adjectives** are *this, that, these,* and *those.*
This and *that* point out one person, place, or thing.

   this skater   **that judge**

These and *those* point out more than one person, place, or thing.

   these skaters   **those judges**

This and *these* name persons, places, or things that are near.

   this costume next to me   **these skates in my hand**

That and *those* name persons, places, or things that are far.

   that costume in the closet   **those skates on the shelf**

A. Circle the correct demonstrative adjective in parentheses.

1. In pair skating (this (these)) two compete regularly.
2. ((That) Those) skating outfit is a beautiful color.
3. The sequins on (that (those)) blouses glitter in the lights.
4. Having matching outfits makes ((that) those) pair look stylish.
5. ((This) These) pair of skates matches the sequined outfit perfectly.
6. For jumps on the ice, ((these) this) skates have toe picks.
7. ((That) Those) couple does ice dancing.
8. In their routine (that (those)) skaters can't do lifts.
9. Fast-moving music keeps (this (these)) two skating quickly.
10. ((This) These) type of skating looks like ballroom dancing.

B. Complete each sentence with the correct demonstrative adjective.

1. Figure skaters use ___[this]___ (near) type of skate.
2. ___[These]___ (near) skates have teeth cut in the front of the blade.
3. Spins and figures are made with ___[these]___ (near) toe picks.
4. Also, the bottom of ___[these]___ (near) skates is curved.
5. ___[That]___ (far) skate is used just for speed skating.
6. ___[Those]___ (far) skate boots are inexpensive and lightweight.
7. Steel tubing reinforces ___[those]___ (far) thin, flat blades.
8. The blades and boots on ___[those]___ (far) skates are designed for speed.
9. ___[These]___ (near) ice-hockey skates have very heavy boots.
10. Players get support and protection from ___[that]___ (far) shoe.

42. Using Possessive Adjectives

A **possessive adjective** shows possession or ownership. The possessive adjectives are *my, your, his, her, its, our, your,* and *their*.

SINGULAR	**my necklace**	**your sandwich**	**his/her/its bowl**
PLURAL	**our footballs**	**your sweaters**	**their magazines**

A **contraction** is made by joining two words. A contraction has an apostrophe. A possessive adjective does not have an apostrophe.

POSSESSIVE ADJECTIVE	**its**	**your**	**their**
CONTRACTION	**it's (it is)**	**you're (you are)**	**they're (they are)**

A. Underline the possessive adjective in each sentence.

1. <u>Our</u> class had <u>its</u> own Olympics.

2. Everyone kept <u>his</u> own score.

3. The events tested <u>your</u> silliness.

4. We paddled <u>our</u> skateboards with plungers.

5. I had trouble keeping <u>my</u> feet on the skateboard.

6. Walking a floor balance beam, Teresa kept the book on <u>her</u> head.

7. Kate leaned <u>her</u> forehead on the upright bat and walked around it.

8. Afterwards she had trouble with <u>her</u> balance.

9. How high can you count with a pencil between <u>your</u> nose and top lip?

10. The boys were able to hold pencils behind <u>their</u> ears better than the girls were.

B. Circle the correct word in parentheses.

1. (Their) They're) reasons for not winning were many.

2. The stick and (its) it's) plunger did not stay together.

3. (Your (You're)) sure they didn't use glue?

4. (They're (Their)) lips were certainly sticky!

5. (Your) You're) ears are bigger than mine.

6. (Its (It's)) not my fault that my feet come in that size!

7. (Their (They're)) dizzy from walking around the bat.

8. (Its (It's)) your fault that the bat broke.

9. You won because (your) you're) voice is louder than mine!

10. This was not (your) you're) typical contest.

Name_____

43. Using Adjectives That Tell How Many

Some adjectives tell how many or about how many.

SINGULAR	PLURAL	SINGULAR	PLURAL
tenth inning	ten innings	either man	most men
each athlete	all athletes	little time	few minutes
neither boy	both boys	much popcorn	many peanuts
every girl	some girls	any child	any children
another runner	several runners		

A. Underline the adjectives that tell how many. Do not include articles.

1. The pentathlon is a competition of five events.
2. The events are held in one day.
3. The first event is the long jump.
4. Throwing the javelin is the second test.
5. Before throwing the javelin, the athlete takes several steps.
6. Each athlete must also throw a discus.
7. A discus is a round metal or wooden object weighing four pounds.
8. An athlete holds it in one hand and spins around before releasing it.
9. A decathlon has ten events.
10. It is held over a period of two days.

B. Complete each sentence with an adjective that tells how many.
Do not include articles. [Possible answers are given.]

1. The Winter Olympics are held every __[four]__ years.
2. A gold medal is the __[first]__ prize.
3. The __[second]__ prize is a silver medal.
4. A bronze medal is given as a __[third]__ prize.
5. There are __[five]__ rings on the Olympic flag.
6. __[Many]__ countries have representative athletes.
7. __[Most]__ athletes are proud just to be there.
8. __[All]__ members of teams receive individual medals.
9. __[Every]__ country should be proud of its athletes.
10. __[All]__ athletes and coaches march in the parade.

Adjectives

44. Recognizing the Position of Adjectives

An adjective usually comes before the noun it modifies.

delicate flower   **shiny penny**

When an adjective follows a verb of being, it is a subject complement. It completes the meaning of the verb and describes the subject of the sentence.

The flower is delicate.   **The penny is shiny.**

A. Underline the descriptive adjectives.

1. A thick mitt helps the catcher.

2. Thinner gloves are used by the basemen.

3. The strong mask protects the face of the catcher.

4. The outfielder runs slowly on the muddy field.

5. The gloves are made from genuine leather.

B. Underline the subject complement in each sentence.

1. The catcher's mitt is thick.

2. Basemen's gloves are thinner.

3. The catcher's mask is strong.

4. The field is muddy.

5. The leather in baseball gloves is genuine.

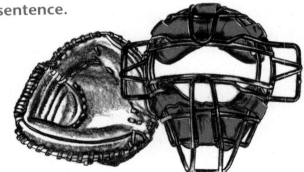

C. Underline the adjectives that come before nouns. Circle the subject complements.

1. The old baseball was (dirty) and (worn.)

2. The thread around the corky center is (blue) and (gray.)

3. Under the thread the black and red material is (rubbery.)

4. The leathery cover is (smooth.)

5. The precious signature on it is (blurry.)

45. Forming the Comparative and Superlative Forms of Adjectives

> An adjective in the **positive degree** describes one or more persons, places, or things.
>
> **Tom is <u>tall</u>.   Bill and Sally are <u>intelligent</u>.**
>
> The **comparative degree** compares two persons, places, or things.
> Form comparative adjectives by adding *-er* to the positive degree or by putting *more* before the positive degree.
>
> **Tom is <u>taller</u> than Sara.   Sally is <u>more intelligent</u> than Tom.**
>
> The **superlative degree** compares three or more persons, places, or things.
> Form superlative adjectives by adding *-est* to the positive degree or by putting *most* before the positive degree.
>
> **Sara is the <u>shortest</u> person in her family.**
> **She is also the <u>most intelligent</u> person in her family.**

A. On the line write **P** if the phrase is positive, **C** if it is comparative degree, or **S** if it is superlative degree.

___[S]___ 1. loudest yell   ___[C]___ 6. higher kick

___[P]___ 2. graceful jab   ___[P]___ 7. careless slap

___[S]___ 3. latest class   ___[S]___ 8. smoothest move

___[P]___ 4. tiny child   ___[C]___ 9. whiter robe

___[C]___ 5. faster runner   ___[C]___ 10. quicker punch

B. Complete each sentence with the adjective in the correct degree of comparison.

early—*superlative*
1. Karate is one of the ____[earliest]____ forms of unarmed combat.

close—*superlative*
2. "Open hand" is the ____[closest]____ translation of the word *karate*.

familiar—*superlative*
3. I am ____[most familiar]____ with Chinese karate, kung fu, which stresses circular hand movements.

powerful—*comparative*
4. Korean karate, tae kwon do, uses ____[more powerful]____ kicking movements.

safe—*positive*
5. The ____[safe]____ use of karate is for self-defense.

Name_____

46. Reviewing Adjectives

A. Complete the paragraph by writing the appropriate adjectives on the lines.

spicy   juicy   fresh   crisp   creamy

flaky   chilled   crunchy   stuffed   delicious

[Possible answers are given.]

Athletes from various countries sat together and ate a __[delicious]__ meal.
1.

They began with a __[crisp]__ salad and a __[chilled]__ fruit cup with a
2.   3.

__[creamy]__ sauce. They shared __[spicy]__ pizza slices, __[juicy]__
4.   5.   6.

hamburgers, tacos in __[crunchy]__ shells, and __[stuffed]__ baked potatoes.
               7.   8.

Picking only one of the __[flaky]__ French pastries was difficult. The athletes
              9.

seemed to drink gallons of __[fresh]__ milk. Friendships were formed during
              10.

this meal.

B. Write the proper adjective for the country that is famous for each type of food.

1. __[Italian]__ spaghetti (Italy)
2. __[Belgian]__ waffles (Belgium)
3. __[French]__ pastries (France)
4. __[Chinese]__ chop suey (China)
5. __[German]__ potato salad (Germany)
6. __[Polish]__ sausage (Poland)
7. __[Mexican]__ enchiladas (Mexico)
8. __[Swiss]__ fondue (Switzerland)
9. __[Japanese]__ sushi (Japan)
10. __[Hungarian]__ goulash (Hungary)

C. Complete each sentence with the correct article.

1. __[An]__ athlete must eat a balanced diet.
2. __[A]__ balanced diet is important to his training.
3. Eating correctly provides her body with __[the]__ energy to compete.
4. She always eats __[a]__ piece of fruit as a snack.
5. __[The]__ fruit gives her a lot of energy.

CONTINUED

D. Complete each sentence with the correct demonstrative adjective.

1. " [These] (*near*) apples look good," thought Sadako.
2. She'd like a slice of [that] (*far*) watermelon.
3. Her brother wants some of [those] (*far*) cherries.
4. [This] (*near*) cantaloupe smells ripe.
5. [Those] (*far*) grapes look delicious.

E. On the line write **P** if the *italicized* adjective is positive, **C** if it is comparative degree, or **S** if it is superlative degree.

[P] 1. Sadako believed in signs of *good* luck.
[P] 2. She looked forward to a *great* race.
[C] 3. Her *older* brother encouraged her.
[S] 4. He said she would be the *fastest* runner.
[C] 5. Sadako knew she was *better* than she had been last year.

F. Complete each sentence with a subject complement. [Possible answers are given.]

1. Sadako was [nervous] before the race.
2. Her legs were [thin] but powerful.
3. When she won, Sadako was [happy].
4. Her friends were [proud] of her.
5. "Sadako always was [fast]," said her father.

Try It Yourself

Write three sentences about your favorite meal. Be sure to use adjectives correctly.

_____

_____

_____

Check Your Own Work

Choose a selection from your writing portfolio, your journal, a work in progress, an assignment from another class, or a letter. Revise it, applying the skills you have reviewed. The checklist will help you.

✔ Have you capitalized all proper adjectives?

✔ Have you used *a* and *an* correctly?

✔ Do your demonstrative adjectives agree with their nouns?

✔ Have you used each adjective in the correct degree?

Adjectives

Name _____

47. Recognizing Action Verbs

> An **action verb** is a word used to express action.
>
> **Tom <u>opened</u> his birthday presents.**

A. Circle the action verb in each sentence.

1. Bobby (studies) every day after school.

2. Sometimes he (works) on a project with a friend.

3. Yesterday his science teacher (gave) the class an assignment.

4. Bobby (visited) his new friend John.

5. The boys (performed) the science experiment.

6. John (went) to the kitchen for a snack.

7. He (returned) with two glasses of lemonade.

8. Then the kitchen door (opened) again.

9. John (came) in with some cookies.

10. But John already (stood) beside Bobby with the lemonade!

B. Complete each sentence with an action verb. **[Possible answers are given.]**

1. Bobby _____[gasped]_____ in astonishment.

2. He _____[looked]_____ from one boy to the other.

3. He _____[waved]_____ his hand before his eyes.

4. He _____[thought]_____ he must have studied too long.

5. Sometimes your eyes _____[play]_____ tricks on you.

6. Bobby _____[jumped]_____ to his feet.

7. John _____[explained]_____ that the other boy was his twin.

8. He _____[introduced]_____ Bobby and Jason.

9. Bobby _____[laughed]_____ at their joke.

10. "You _____[fooled]_____ me!" he said.

Name_____

48. Using Action Verbs

A. Complete each sentence with an action verb. [Possible answers are given.]

1. Mr. and Mrs. Joyce ____[went]____ to the pound to get a dog.
2. The happy puppy ____[wagged]____ its tail when it saw the children.
3. Claire ____[named]____ the dog Coco.
4. Sean ____[made]____ a bed for the puppy.
5. Sean and Claire ____[take]____ turns feeding Coco.
6. Sean ____[walks]____ the puppy after school every day.
7. Yesterday he ____[played]____ with Coco at the park.
8. There she ____[dug]____ a hole to bury her toy.
9. She always ____[barks]____ at strangers.
10. Coco ____[chews]____ on socks if they are on the floor.
11. Sometimes she ____[chases]____ squirrels up a tree.
12. Coco ____[wakes]____ Claire every morning by tugging her blankets.
13. She ____[throws]____ Coco a ball.
14. Coco ____[catches]____ it every time!
15. At the end of the day, Coco ____[sleeps]____ in her own bed.

B. Write a sentence using each verb. [Sentences will vary.]

giggle 1. _____
tumble 2. _____
ride 3. _____
play 4. _____
jog 5. _____
grasp 6. _____
scream 7. _____
tickle 8. _____
jump 9. _____
nap 10. _____

Verbs

49. Writing Action Verbs

A. Write an action verb that each person, animal, or thing can perform.
[Possible answers are given.]

1. puppies _____[eat]_____
2. birds _____[fly]_____
3. children _____[talk]_____
4. students _____[study]_____
5. rock groups _____[sing]_____
6. authors _____[write]_____
7. babies _____[laugh]_____
8. athletes _____[jump]_____
9. cows _____[graze]_____
10. boats _____[float]_____

11. flowers _____[bloom]_____
12. horses _____[gallop]_____
13. cars _____[crash]_____
14. balloons _____[burst]_____
15. clocks _____[tick]_____
16. tires _____[screech]_____
17. bunnies _____[hop]_____
18. fish _____[swim]_____
19. dishes _____[break]_____
20. windows _____[shatter]_____

B. Complete each sentence with a verb from the list. Use each word once.

cried	yelled	asked	whispered	responded
called	questioned	exclaimed	gasped	replied

1. "Oh no!" _____[gasped]_____ Molly. [Answers will vary.]

2. "My rabbit's cage door is open, and I don't see him!"

   she _____[cried]_____.

3. She _____[yelled]_____ for her sister.

4. "Have you seen Fluffy?" _____[asked]_____ Molly.

5. Hannah _____[responded]_____, "No, but I'll help you find him."

6. They _____[called]_____, "Fluffy, come here, Fluffy."

7. After looking for hours, Hannah _____[exclaimed]_____,
   "There he is, sleeping!"

8. "How sweet!" Molly _____[whispered]_____ so she wouldn't wake him.

9. "What should we do?" _____[questioned]_____ Hannah.

10. Molly _____[replied]_____, "Let's let him sleep."

Name_____

50. Identifying Verbs of Being

> A **being verb** is a word used to express existence. The most common being verbs are *is, are, was, were, be, been,* and *being*.

A. Circle the being verb in each sentence. If the being verb has a helping verb, circle the entire verb.

1. Traveling (is) a lot of fun.
2. I (have been) on many trips.
3. My trip to Utah (was) incredible.
4. We (were) alone in the desert under millions of stars.
5. The many stars (were) our tiny personal lanterns.
6. I (have been) to several U.S. national parks.
7. The hiking trails (will be) open soon in Grand Teton National Park.
8. The trails (were) not open last fall because of the snow.
9. It (has been) a long time since I have hiked in the mountains.
10. I hear that you (will be) in Rome soon.
11. Rome (has been) on my list of places to go for a long time.
12. There (are) so many beautiful churches there.
13. The Vatican Museum (is) full of famous works by Michelangelo and Raphael.
14. The Sistine Chapel ceiling (has been) famous for centuries.
15. There (are) many wonderful countries, cities, and landscapes to see and explore.

B. Underline the being verbs in the paragraph.

Venice has been on my list of Italian cities to visit. There are few streets in Venice, but there are many canals. The biggest one is the Grand Canal. It has been the "Main Street" of Venice for a long time. The center of activity is St. Mark's Square. This is a large area near St. Mark's Cathedral. People will be there even late at night. In Venice, boats are the chief means of transportation. The gondola is a famous kind of Venetian boat. Its movement is from an oar controlled by a gondolier. Gondoliers have been the operators of these boats for centuries. Nowadays gondolas are mainly for tourists. Boats with motors are the principal means of transportation. Venice will always be an interesting and unusual city to visit.

Verbs

54

51. Recognizing Verbs and Sentences

> A verb is a very important word in a sentence.
> Every sentence must have a verb.

A. Write **S** before each group of words that is a sentence.
Write **NS** before each group of words that needs a verb.

__[NS]__ 1. The crab on the sandy beach.

__[S]__ 2. I like to collect seashells.

__[S]__ 3. Don't swim too far.

__[NS]__ 4. The hot yellow sun.

__[NS]__ 5. A flock of noisy seagulls overhead.

__[NS]__ 6. A ship off in the distance.

__[S]__ 7. Waves rolled onto the shore.

__[NS]__ 8. A lot of interesting shells.

__[S]__ 9. A turtle scampered into the water.

__[NS]__ 10. The sunlight on the water.

__[S]__ 11. After putting down our towels, we ran to the water.

__[S]__ 12. In the afternoon we built two sand castles.

__[S]__ 13. A tunnel connected the sand castles.

__[NS]__ 14. A huge foamy wave.

__[S]__ 15. It was fun to play paddleball on the beach.

B. Add an action verb and additional words to form sentences. **[Sentences will vary.]**

1. Many happy children _____

2. A strong wind _____

3. A colorful, striped umbrella _____

4. The mothers on the shore _____

5. The lifeguard in the boat _____

Verbs

52. Recognizing Verb Phrases

A **verb phrase** is a group of words that does the work of a single verb.
A verb phrase contains one or more auxiliary, or helping, verbs *(is, are, has, have, will, can, could, would, should, etc.)* and a main verb.

Regular exercise is needed for good health.
He could have improved his health by hiking.

Underline the verb phrase in each sentence. Write on the lines the auxiliary verb(s) and the principal verb.

	AUXILIARY VERB	PRINCIPAL VERB
1. In the spring he will hike the Appalachian Trail.	[will]	[hike]
2. The Appalachian Trail is also named the A.T.	[is]	[named]
3. Hiking the trail from end to end is called thru-hiking.	[is]	[called]
4. A thru-hiker will cross 2,100 miles.	[will]	[cross]
5. The trail has been marked with blazes.	[has been]	[marked]
6. White rectangular marks have been painted on trees.	[have been]	[painted]
7. Blazes can help hikers from becoming lost.	[can]	[help]
8. Hikers should make camp before sundown.	[should]	[make]
9. On the A.T. one can find shelters a day's hike apart.	[can]	[find]
10. Many people have camped along the trail.	[have]	[camped]
11. Porcupines were sighted near the campsite.	[were]	[sighted]
12. Black bears have appeared along the trail.	[have]	[appeared]
13. One should leave no trace after using a campsite.	[should]	[leave]
14. You should visit the A.T. once in your lifetime.	[should]	[visit]
15. Thousands of people will hike the trail this year.	[will]	[hike]

Verbs

Name_____

53. Recognizing Verb Phrases in Questions and Negative Statements

In questions and negative statements the auxiliary verb and the main verb may be separated.

Will you come to the party tonight?   They are not expected to be there.

A. Underline the principal verb and the auxiliary verb in each sentence.

1. Do you like dogs?
2. Carlos does not own a dog.
3. Do Dalmatians have spots?
4. Has Frisky been to the veterinarian yet?
5. Frisky did not receive the vaccination.
6. Can Great Danes grow that tall?
7. Was Frisky walked after school?
8. My dog does not bark often.
9. Poodles do not shed much.
10. Did Bandit dig that hole in the yard?
11. What do English foxhounds like to hunt?
12. Can your dog jump over the fence?
13. Do you brush your Old English sheepdog often in the summer?
14. Can your Saint Bernard fit through the door?
15. Were chows used for hunting?

B. Answer each question with a negative response. Underline the principal verb and the auxiliary verb in the question and the response.

1. Did you watch the late movie last night?

    [I did not watch the late movie last night.] _____

2. May she go to the movies tonight?

    [She may not go to the movies tonight.] _____

3. Should we watch the film at nine o'clock?

    [We should not watch the film at nine o'clock.] _____

4. Will you buy popcorn for the show?

    [I will not buy popcorn for the show.] _____

5. Are they paying for the show themselves?

    [They are not paying for the show themselves.] _____

54. Identifying Regular and Irregular Verbs

A verb has four principal parts: the present, the present participle, the past, and the past participle. The present participle is formed by adding *-ing* to the present form of the verb. The simple past and past participle of regular verbs are formed by adding *-ed* or *-d* to the present. The simple past and the past participle of irregular verbs do not end in *-ed* or *-d*.

PRESENT	PRESENT PARTICIPLE	PAST	PAST PARTICIPLE
talk	talking	talked	talked
hop	hopping	hopped	hopped
smile	smiling	smiled	smiled
drink	drinking	drank	drunk
hit	hitting	hit	hit
hide	hiding	hid	hidden

A. Write the present participle, the past, and the past participle of each verb.

	PRESENT PARTICIPLE	PAST	PAST PARTICIPLE
1. cheer	[cheering]	[cheered]	[cheered]
2. sigh	[sighing]	[sighed]	[sighed]
3. play	[playing]	[played]	[played]
4. make	[making]	[made]	[made]
5. fall	[falling]	[fell]	[fallen]
6. roll	[rolling]	[rolled]	[rolled]
7. do	[doing]	[did]	[done]
8. rise	[rising]	[rose]	[risen]
9. hop	[hopping]	[hopped]	[hopped]
10. write	[writing]	[wrote]	[written]

B. Write **R** on the line if the verb is regular or **I** if the verb is irregular.

1. talk [R]
2. push [R]
3. come [I]
4. hurt [I]
5. serve [R]
6. teach [I]
7. look [R]

8. know [I]
9. grow [I]
10. carry [R]
11. explore [R]
12. see [I]
13. do [I]
14. compare [R]

15. take [I]
16. smile [R]
17. sink [I]
18. lay [I]
19. stand [I]
20. skip [R]

Verbs

Name_____

55. Recognizing Regular and Irregular Verbs

> The simple past and past participle of regular verbs end in *-ed* or *-d*.
> The simple past and past participles of irregular verbs do not end in *-ed* or *-d*.

A. Underline the verb or verb phrase in each sentence. Write **R** on the line if the principal verb is regular or **I** if it is irregular.

___[I]___ 1. Recently our class <u>took</u> a trip to the Vietnam War Memorial.

___[R]___ 2. The memorial is <u>located</u> in Washington, D.C.

___[I]___ 3. It was <u>built</u> in honor of those who served in Vietnam.

___[I]___ 4. The names of all the dead <u>are written</u> in stone.

___[R]___ 5. Family members and friends often <u>visit</u> the memorial.

___[I]___ 6. Some <u>find</u> the name of a deceased loved one.

___[I]___ 7. Often they <u>leave</u> flowers at the site.

___[I]___ 8. The flowers <u>are</u> a sign of remembrance.

___[I]___ 9. The memorial <u>makes</u> a lasting impression on each visitor.

___[R]___ 10. We <u>have learned</u> to appreciate the sacrifices of those who served.

B. Write a sentence using each verb. Write **R** on the line if the verb is regular or **I** if it is irregular. **[Sentences will vary.]**

___[I]___ 1. took _____

___[I]___ 2. ate _____

___[R]___ 3. laughed _____

___[R]___ 4. walked _____

___[R]___ 5. studied _____

___[I]___ 6. made _____

___[R]___ 7. answered _____

___[I]___ 8. knew _____

___[R]___ 9. painted _____

___[R]___ 10. talk _____

Name_____

56. Writing Regular and Irregular Verbs

A. Complete each sentence with the simple past or the past participle of the verb. Remember to use the past participle if the sentence has an auxiliary verb.

fall   1. How much rain has _____[fallen]_____ here this year?

study   2. Scientists have _____[studied]_____ rainfall for years.

collect   3. The rain is _____[collected]_____ in a bucket.

stop   4. When the rain has _____[stopped]_____, the scientists measure the depth.

make   5. They have _____[made]_____ studies of the weather cycle from the results.

be   6. Rain has always _____[been]_____ an important source of fresh water.

cause   7. Today air pollutants have _____[caused]_____ some rainwater to be unhealthful.

result   8. Many human activities have also _____[resulted]_____ in polluted water.

find   9. Polluted water has been _____[found]_____ to be dangerous to human health.

learn   10. We have _____[learned]_____ that polluted water can make us sick.

B. Complete each sentence with the simple past or the past participle of the verb.

eat   1. Mike had _____[eaten]_____ his breakfast early that day.

grow   2. The plant _____[grew]_____ two inches.

give   3. I had _____[given]_____ my catcher's mitt to my friend.

go   4. Who _____[went]_____ to the game yesterday?

throw   5. The outfielder _____[threw]_____ the ball to the catcher.

teach   6. Our teacher had _____[taught]_____ us how to add fractions.

display   7. Harold _____[displayed]_____ the population data in a circle graph.

try   8. We _____[tried]_____ that solution to the equation.

jump   9. The athlete _____[jumped]_____ rope for exercise.

stand   10. The fans _____[stood]_____ in line for the concert tickets.

Verbs

60

57. Using Forms of Break and See

> The principal parts of the verb *break* and *see* are as follows:
>
> | PRESENT | PRESENT PARTICIPLE | PAST | PAST PARTICIPLE |
> |---------|--------------------|------|-----------------|
> | **break** | **breaking** | **broke** | **broken** |
> | **see** | **seeing** | **saw** | **seen** |
>
> The present participle is always used with a helping verb such as *is, are, was,* or *were.*
> The past participle is always used with a helping verb such as *has, have,* or *had.*

A. Complete each sentence with a correct form of the verb *break.*

1. _____[Break]_____ the news to her slowly.

2. You might _____[break]_____ her heart with the news.

3. Someone has _____[broken]_____ your china serving plate.

4. Who _____[broke]_____ it?

5. Would anyone _____[break]_____ it on purpose?

6. My grandmother used this for sixty years and never _____[broke]_____ it.

7. I have _____[broken]_____ things but never anything so precious.

8. Why couldn't you _____[break]_____ a cheap cereal bowl?

9. Like Humpty Dumpty, this plate is _____[broken]_____ and can't be fixed.

10. Who has not _____[broken]_____ something and been disappointed?

B. Complete each sentence with a correct form of the verb *see.*

1. Yesterday at the play, I _____[saw]_____ something that scared me.

2. In the story *A Christmas Carol,* Scrooge _____[saw/sees]_____ Marley's ghost.

3. When I _____[saw]_____ Marley on stage, I was frightened.

4. I'm afraid I'll _____[see]_____ him in my sleep.

5. I told you what you have _____[seen]_____ is fiction.

6. You have _____[seen]_____ ghosts on TV, and you weren't afraid.

7. But I have never _____[seen]_____ one like Marley before.

8. Well, you will never _____[see]_____ one in your own bedroom.

9. I know someone who _____[saw]_____ one in her bedroom.

10. I think some people are _____[seeing]_____ things that aren't there.

Verbs

Name_____

58. Using Forms of Go and Choose

> The principal parts of the *go* and *choose* are as follows:
>
> | PRESENT | PRESENT PARTICIPLE | PAST | PAST PARTICIPLE |
> |---------|--------------------|------|-----------------|
> | go | going | went | gone |
> | choose | choosing | chose | chosen |
>
> The present participle is always used with a helping verb such as *is, are, was,* or *were.*
> The past participle is always used with a helping verb such as *has, have,* or *had.*

A. Complete each sentence with a correct form of the verb *go.*

1. Mrs. Henry's students ____[go]____ on a class trip every year.

2. Have the students ____[gone]____ on their trip yet this year?

3. Last week they ____[went]____ to a museum.

4. The students were ____[going]____ to see the mummies first.

5. Had Mark ever ____[gone]____ to a museum before?

6. Maya accidentally ____[went]____ to the wrong exhibit.

7. The students ____[went]____ back to the bus at six o'clock.

8. By that time the tour guides were ____[going]____ home.

9. Jean hopes she can ____[go]____ back next year.

10. Mrs. Henry has ____[gone]____ to the museum many times.

B. Complete each sentence with a correct form of the verb *choose.*

1. Please ____[choose]____ any book you wish to read.

2. Each boy is ____[choosing]____ his favorite story.

3. Yesterday I ____[chose]____ a book with a fairy on the cover.

4. The author usually ____[chooses]____ to write about magical places.

5. Has the teacher ____[chosen]____ a book to read in class?

6. He has always ____[chosen]____ good books before.

7. Last week he ____[chose]____ *Old Yeller.*

8. The class had ____[chosen]____ to hear that book.

9. Which book are you ____[choosing]____?

10. I have ____[chosen]____ one about a man who hiked the entire Appalachian Trail.

Verbs

Name_____

59. Using Forms of Take

The principal parts of the *take* are as follows:

PRESENT	PRESENT PARTICIPLE	PAST	PAST PARTICIPLE
take	taking	took	taken

The present participle is always used with a helping verb such as *is, are, was,* or *were.*
The past participle is always used with a helping verb such as *has, have,* or *had.*

A. Complete each sentence with a correct form of the verb *take.*

1. I ____[took]____ your temperature, and you are fine.

2. Then can you ____[take]____ me to the gym?

3. ____[Take]____ your things, and we'll go.

4. Rudy has already ____[taken]____ the equipment to the gym.

5. I wish he had ____[taken]____ my headache too.

6. I hope he is ____[taking]____ my gym shoes, because I don't see them.

7. Have you ____[taken]____ some medicine for your headache?

8. ____[Take]____ an aspirin, or you'll feel terrible at the gym.

9. I ____[took]____ the last one yesterday.

10. Well, then I hope you can ____[take]____ the pain today.

B. Circle the correct form of the verb *take* in parentheses.

1. Little Mary was (taking) took) the scissors off the table.

2. She (take (took)) them to cut out a paper doll.

3. Jack quickly (taken (took)) the sharp scissors from her.

4. Why did you (take) taken) those?

5. I (take (took)) them because they are dangerous.

6. You shouldn't have (took (taken)) such sharp scissors.

7. I will (take) took) the scissors and cut out the doll for you.

8. (Take) Took) this piece of paper for the doll.

9. I (take (took)) that piece of paper already.

10. Are you (taking) took) this paper doll to school?

60. Using Verb Tenses

The simple past tense does not have an auxiliary verb in statements.
I went to Harper School last year.
Use the past participle with a form of the auxiliary verb *have* (*has, have, had*).
I have gone to Lincoln School since September.

A. Complete each sentence with the simple past or past participle of the verb.

sit 1. The campers ____[sat]____ around the campfire.

sing 2. They ____[sang]____ folk songs until midnight.

roast 3. We ____[roasted]____ marshmallows.

climb 4. Her cousin has ____[climbed]____ rocks in Yosemite National Park.

experience 5. In 1997 Yosemite ____[experienced]____ its greatest flooding in more than a century.

cover 6. Five feet of water ____[covered]____ the campgrounds.

repair 7. The park has ____[repaired]____ most of the damage.

fall 8. Leaves ____[fell]____ to the ground like a colorful blanket.

bring 9. We ____[brought]____ water-purification tablets.

stand 10. The mountain ____[stood]____ high above the treetops.

hike 11. Carlos and his family have ____[hiked]____ along the Grand Canyon's rim.

catch 12. Natalie ____[caught]____ a trout in the Bald River.

spend 13. They ____[spent]____ two nights in the forest.

see 14. We have ____[seen]____ tundra swans and bald eagles in the wildlife refuge.

take 15. Michael has ____[taken]____ dozens of pictures of them.

B. Write a sentence using each verb or verb phrase. [Sentences will vary.]

has hurt 1. _____

bought 2. _____

have seen 3. _____

sank 4. _____

drank 5. _____

Name_____

61. Recognizing Simple Verb Tenses

The **tense of a verb** shows the time of its action. There are three simple tenses. The simple present tense tells about something that is always true or about an action that happens again and again. The simple past tense tells about an action that happened in the past. The simple future tells about an action that will happen.

SIMPLE PRESENT   **The children play games at recess.**

SIMPLE PAST   **They played quietly for an hour.**

SIMPLE FUTURE   **They will play softball tomorrow.**

Underline the verb or verb phrase in each sentence. Write the tense on the line.

_____[present]_____   1. Many years after her death, Dorothea Dix still lives in history books.

_____[past]_____   2. Dorothea spent much of her life in Maine and Massachusetts.

_____[past]_____   3. She carried the heartache of an unhappy childhood throughout her life.

_____[present]_____   4. Dorothea presents an image of a teacher in the early 1800s.

_____[past]_____   5. At age 14 she founded a school for young children.

_____[past]_____   6. Dorothea learned of the problems of the sick, the poor, and the insane.

_____[past]_____   7. She devoted her life to their care.

_____[present]_____   8. The sick, the poor, and the insane still need help today.

_____[future]_____   9. Where will they find this help?

_____[past]_____   10. She investigated hospitals' treatment of the sick and the insane.

_____[past]_____   11. With a rich friend's help, Dorothea built a state hospital in New Jersey.

_____[past]_____   12. In Europe she educated nurses on patient care.

_____[future]_____   13. Because of Dorothea nurses will continue the study of all aspects of hospital care.

_____[present]_____   14. Only a very generous person volunteers free service to others.

_____[present]_____   15. Dorothea's epitaph describes her as the most useful and distinguished woman in America.

Dorothea Dix believed in helping the sick and the insane, so she fought for their rights. How can you help someone who is sick? Give an example.

65

Name_____

62. Recognizing Progressive Verb Tenses

> The present progressive tense tells what is happening now.
> The present progressive tense is formed with the present participle and a present form of the verb *be (am, is, are)*.
>
> **He is riding his bike in the park.**
>
> The past progressive tense tells what was happening in the past.
> The past progressive tense is formed with the present participle and a past form of the verb *be (was, were)*.
>
> **He was riding his bike when the accident happened.**

Underline the verb phrase in each sentence.
Write the tense on the line.

1. We <u>are</u> all <u>having</u> a great day. [present progressive]

2. The sun <u>is shining</u>. [present progressive]

3. Birds <u>are singing</u> in the trees. [present progressive]

4. It <u>was raining</u> a while ago. [past progressive]

5. Bushes and trees <u>were swaying</u> in the strong wind. [past progressive]

6. Now <u>I'm strolling</u> through the park. [present progressive]

7. Children <u>are playing</u> on the swings. [present progressive]

8. People <u>are eating</u> their lunches in the sunshine. [present progressive]

9. They <u>were huddling</u> under their umbrellas before. [past progressive]

10. Now everyone <u>is enjoying</u> the nice weather. [present progressive]

11. Yesterday at this time I <u>was sitting</u> in school. [past progressive]

12. The teacher <u>was explaining</u> the movements of planets. [past progressive]

13. They <u>are</u> all <u>revolving</u> around the sun. [present progressive]

14. They <u>are</u> also <u>rotating</u> on their axes. [present progressive]

15. Some students <u>were making</u> a model of the solar system. [past progressive]

Verbs

66

63. Recognizing Transitive Verbs

A **transitive verb** expresses an action that passes from a doer to a receiver.

      Doer   **Receiver**

The **kitten** climbed the **tree**.

The receiver is the direct object of the verb.

                    Direct object

The **kitten** climbed the **tree**.

A. Underline the transitive verb in each sentence.
Write the direct object on the line.

  [kitten]   1. A fireman <u>rescued</u> the kitten.

  [ladder]   2. He <u>placed</u> the ladder against the tree.

  [ladder]   3. He <u>climbed</u> the ladder quickly.

 [branches]   4. He <u>grabbed</u> some branches.

  [tree]   5. This <u>shook</u> the tree.

  [trunk]   6. He <u>hugged</u> its trunk to steady himself.

  [paw]   7. He bent down and <u>touched</u> a paw.

  [paw]   8. The kitten <u>pulled</u> her paw away.

  [hand]   9. Then she <u>scratched</u> his hand.

  [hand]   10. He <u>shook</u> his hand in pain.

  [kitten]   11. Should he <u>grab</u> the kitten now?

 [chance]   12. He would <u>take</u> the chance.

  [kitten]   13. Finally he <u>held</u> the kitten in his arms.

  [cheek]   14. The kitten <u>licked</u> his cheek and purred.

  [hand]   15. The kitten's owner <u>shook</u> the fireman's hand in thanks.

B. Complete each sentence with a direct object. **[Possible answers are given.]**

1. Babies eat _____[applesauce]_____.

2. They are happy when they see their _____[mothers]_____.

3. A baby's mother always carries _____[milk]_____ with her.

4. She has to buy _____[diapers]_____ quite often.

5. The baby will grab your _____[hair]_____ if you are close enough.

64. Recognizing Intransitive Verbs

> An **intransitive verb** has no receiver of the action.
> It does not have a direct object.
>
> **The jewels sparkled on her neck.**

A. Circle the intransitive verb in each sentence. Underline the doer of the action.

1. The dire <u>wolf</u> (lived) in western North America hundreds of thousands of years ago.

2. Now the gray <u>wolf</u> (travels) across parts of Canada and Alaska.

3. The gray <u>wolf</u> (grows) very large, sometimes to six and a half feet long.

4. Your pet <u>dog</u> (descended) from a gray wolf.

5. These <u>wolves</u> (hunt) at night.

6. <u>They</u> (thrive) on deer, moose, and caribou.

7. <u>They</u> (sleep) in dens.

8. Young <u>wolves</u> (remain) with the pack for less than two years.

9. A gray <u>wolf</u> (breeds) between January and April.

10. Red <u>wolves</u>, now endangered, also (exist).

B. Complete each sentence using the verb as an intransitive verb. Circle the intransitive verb in each sentence. **[Answers will vary.]**

1. The ladies chatted _____.

2. The boys argued _____.

3. The fans cheered _____.

4. The people murmured _____.

5. Karl called _____.

6. The coach yelled _____.

7. The students grumbled _____.

8. The birds chirped _____.

9. The little girls giggled _____.

10. The judge and attorneys whispered _____.

65. Identifying Transitive and Intransitive Verbs

A. Write on the line whether the *italicized* verb is transitive or intransitive.

____[intransitive]____ 1. Last summer our family *went* to Disney World.

____[transitive]____ 2. The plane *left* the airport on time.

____[intransitive]____ 3. In the air we *soared* above the clouds.

____[transitive]____ 4. The pilot *landed* the plane smoothly in Florida.

____[transitive]____ 5. At the hotel we *unpacked* our bags.

____[intransitive]____ 6. Hurriedly we *headed* for the park.

____[transitive]____ 7. We *had* so much fun.

____[intransitive]____ 8. All of us *slept* peacefully at the end of the day.

____[transitive]____ 9. We all *had* dreams of the days to come.

____[intransitive]____ 10. Maybe my family *can go* to Disneyland next year.

B. Underline the verb in each sentence. Write **T** on the line if the verb is transitive or **I** if it is intransitive.

___[I]___ 1. The mountaineers <u>rested</u> on the ledge.

___[T]___ 2. They <u>wore</u> crampons on their boots.

___[T]___ 3. Their crampons, sets of spikes attached to the sole of a boot, <u>clutch</u> the ice.

___[I]___ 4. Sherpas <u>trudged</u> behind them.

___[T]___ 5. They <u>carried</u> the supplies.

___[I]___ 6. Sherpas <u>come</u> from Tibet.

___[I]___ 7. Tenzing Norgay, a Sherpa, <u>climbed</u> very well.

___[T]___ 8. He and Edmund Hillary <u>ascended</u> Mount Everest in 1953.

___[I]___ 9. The summit of Everest <u>lies</u> at about 29,000 feet.

___[T]___ 10. The Himalayas <u>offer</u> many challenges to climbers.

Verbs

66. Using Linking Verbs

A **linking verb** links, or joins, a subject with a subject complement that identifies or describes the subject. The subject complement may be a noun, a pronoun, or an adjective. Verbs of being are linking verbs.

NOUN   She *is* the <u>teacher</u> of this class.
PRONOUN   The talented artist *was* <u>he</u>.
ADJECTIVE   The old man behind the counter *was* <u>gruff</u>.

A. Circle the subject complement in each sentence. Write on the line whether it is a noun, a pronoun, or an adjective. The linking verbs are *italicized*.

_____[noun]_____   1. The orange *is* a (fruit) that contains vitamin C.

_____[adjective]_____   2. Those apples *are* (green).

_____[pronoun]_____   3. The fruit vendor *was* (he).

_____[noun]_____   4. Honeydew *is* the (melon) my
                           mother likes least.

_____[adjective]_____   5. The rotten bananas *were* (mushy).

_____[noun]_____   6. These strawberries and blueberries
                           are our (dessert) tonight.

_____[noun]_____   7. Peaches and sugar *are* the main (ingredients) in this pie.

_____[pronoun]_____   8. The best fruit-smoothie maker *is* (she).

_____[noun]_____   9. Those fresh apples *will be* (cobbler) when she is finished with them.

_____[adjective]_____   10. The blueberry pie-eating contest *has* always *been* (fun).

B. Complete each sentence with a subject complement. Use a noun, a pronoun, or an adjective. **[Answers will vary.]**

1. The Art Institute of Chicago is a _____ millions of people
   visit every year.

2. Monet and Picasso are _____ whose works hang in the Art Institute.

3. Water lilies have been the _____ of some of Monet's greatest paintings.

4. The water lilies are _____.

5. Was it not _____ who purchased the painting for a million dollars?

Verbs

67. Understanding the Agreement of Subject and Verb

A subject and a verb always agree in number and person.
Singular nouns and pronouns must have singular verbs.
The third person singular of the simple present tense ends in *-s* or *-es*.

I eat breakfast every day.
You wait for the bus at six o'clock.

The bus wait̲s̲ at the red light.
She eat̲s̲ lunch in the cafeteria.
The cat watch̲e̲s̲ the mouse.

Plural nouns and the plural subject pronouns *we* and *they* must
always have plural verbs. A plural verb does not end in *-s* or *-es*.

Bikers observe traffic laws.
They carry their lunches with them.
We buy the same newspaper every day.

Circle the correct verb form in parentheses. The subject is *italicized*.

1. Each year my *father* (visit (visits)) my grandparents in Ireland.

2. *He* (stay (stays)) two weeks each time.

3. *He* (bring (brings)) pictures of my brothers and me.

4. My *grandfather* ((is) are) always surprised by how much we've grown.

5. My *grandparents* ((take) takes) my father to see relatives.

6. *They* (has (have)) tea and sandwiches.

7. The *tea* ((is) are) made with milk and sugar.

8. My *grandmother* (know (knows)) many old Irish songs.

9. *She* ((is) are) always singing them.

10. My *grandparents* (has (have)) a dog named Shep.

11. My *grandfather* (walk (walks)) to the shore every morning.

12. *People* (is (are)) at work catching lobsters.

13. *Shep* (go (goes)) with my grandfather.

14. A *donkey* ((is) are) in their backyard.

15. My *father* always (bring (brings)) gifts from my grandparents.

68. Using Is, Are, and Am

The forms of the verb *be* in the present tense are *is*, *are*, and *am*. Use *is* when the subject is a singular noun or a third person singular subject pronoun *(he, she, it)*.

> **Chicago is a city with interesting architecture.**
> **She is a great violinist.**

Use *are* when the subject is a plural noun or a first or third person plural subject pronoun *(we, they)*. Use *are* with the second person subject pronoun, *you*.

> **Not many cities are as full of parks as this one.**
> **You are a talented musician.**
> **You are the best athletes in the club.**

Use *am* with the first person subject pronoun, *I*.

> **I am glad to be here.**

A. Circle the correct form of the verb *be* in parentheses.

1. Some of the body's essential nutrients (is (are)) protein, minerals, and vitamins.
2. Some minerals (is (are)) present in the body in just trace amounts.
3. Calcium ((is) are) important for the growth of bones.
4. Potassium ((is) are) a mineral found in potatoes and bananas.
5. Our bodies (is (are)) not able to make vitamins, which we need.
6. Vitamins (is (are)) thought to promote health.
7. The foods we eat (is (are)) made up of protein, carbohydrates, and fats.
8. The cereal you eat in the morning ((is) are) high in carbohydrates.
9. Vegetables (is (are)) good sources of vitamins.
10. Olive oil ((is) are) a fat.

B. Complete each sentence with *is*, *are*, or *am*.

1. Your friends ___[are]___ here.
2. What ___[is]___ keeping you?
3. I ___[am]___ trying to find my keys.
4. I ___[am]___ ready to go now.
5. ___[Are]___ you sure you want to go out in this weather?

Verbs

Name_____

69. Using <u>Was</u> and <u>Were</u>

The forms of the verb *be* in the past tense are *was* and *were*.
Use *was* when the subject is a singular noun or a first or a
third person singular subject pronoun (*I, he, she, it*).

The puppy <u>was</u> playful and frisky.
I <u>was</u> happy to lend her my umbrella.

Use *were* when the subject is a plural noun or a first or a third person
plural subject pronoun (*we, they*). Use *were* with the second person
subject pronoun, *you*.

Ribbons and bows <u>were</u> all over the presents.
You <u>were</u> a great friend.

A. Circle the correct verb in parentheses.

1. (Was Were) Jeff in the science lab with you?
2. (Was Were) you two a team for the project?
3. He (was were) not in the lab yesterday.
4. The samples in the test tubes (was were) green.
5. The teacher (was were) very helpful.
6. The student scientists (was were) disappointed in the results.
7. Those girls with the successful experiment (was were) very proud.
8. The final exam (was were) difficult.
9. (Was Were) all your classmates given the same test?
10. Where (was were) Jeff on test day?

B. Complete each sentence with *was* or *were*.

1. The children ___[were]___ surprised.
2. The clowns ___[were]___ frowning.
3. The magician ___[was]___ in black.
4. The rabbits ___[were]___ in his hat.
5. The trapeze artists ___[were]___ high up in the air.
6. The crowd ___[was]___ silent when the tiger roared.
7. You ___[were]___ afraid until I held your hand.
8. The elephants ___[were]___ giant but gentle.
9. The ringmaster ___[was]___ once a tightrope walker.
10. ___[Were]___ you at the circus too?

70. Using <u>Does</u>, <u>Doesn't</u> and <u>Do</u>, <u>Don't</u>

Use *does* or *doesn't (does not)* when the subject is a singular noun or a third person singular subject pronoun *(he, she, it)*.

> **The striped shirt <u>does</u> go with that plain skirt.**
> **It <u>doesn't</u> seem bright enough in this room.**

Use *do* or *don't (do not)* when the subject is a plural noun or with the subject pronouns *I, we, you,* and *they*.

> **Motorists <u>do</u> like clearly marked street signs.**
> **We <u>don't</u> have the money to go on vacation right now.**

A. Circle the correct verb in parentheses.

1. This chair ((does) do) match the other chairs.

2. ((Doesn't) Don't) this striped velvet look good on it?

3. I (doesn't (don't)) usually like that material.

4. The couch ((does) do) look very comfortable.

5. (Doesn't (Don't)) you like sitting on leather?

6. I (does (do)) like sitting on things that are soft.

7. Velvet ((doesn't) don't) look so bad to me now.

8. Why (doesn't (don't)) we try covering the couch with it?

9. ((Does) do) it cost a fortune?

10. Yes, because we (doesn't (don't)) get it wholesale.

B. Complete each sentence with *does* or *doesn't* or *do* or *don't*.

1. Those curtains ___[do/don't]___ hang gracefully.

2. ___[Do/Don't]___ they have ties to hold them back?

3. One tie ___[does/doesn't]___ work.

4. ___[Does/Doesn't]___ the living room look nice when the curtains are drawn?

5. The sun and the breeze ___[do/don't]___ come in when the curtains are closed.

6. The room ___[does/doesn't]___ look gloomy now.

7. ___[Do/Don't]___ you think the room could use more color?

8. ___[Does/Doesn't]___ that yellow throw pillow cheer things up?

9. One pillow ___[does/doesn't]___ do it.

10. ___[Do/Don't]___ you want to buy some bright fabrics for this room?

Verbs

74

Name_____

71. Using Forms of Let and Leave

The verb *let* (*letting, let, has let*) means "to permit" or "to allow."
> **The babysitter <u>lets</u> the children stay up late.**

The verb *leave* (*leaving, left, has left*) means "to depart" or "to go without taking."
> **If she <u>leaves</u> now, she'll make her train.**
> **Please <u>leave</u> your papers on my desk.**

A. Circle the correct verb in parentheses.

1. Jason will soon (let (leave)) for camp.

2. Paige has ((left) let) already.

3. How soon will you (let (leave))?

4. ((Leave) Let) me help you pack.

5. My brother (let (left)) camp early last year.

6. My mother ((let) left) me bring my radio.

7. The mail carrier (let (left)) without giving the package
   to the camp counselor.

8. The camp counselor would not ((let) left) us swim late at night.

9. I (let (left)) for camp with my sleeping bag and my tent.

10. Will you ((let) left) us roast marshmallows around the campfire tonight?

B. Complete each sentence with a correct form of *let* or *leave*.

1. ___[Let]___ me read your copy of *Sounder.*

2. ___[Leave]___ it on my desk.

3. Don't ___[leave]___ without taking your bookmark.

4. Mother ___[let]___ me read before going to bed.

5. You ___[left]___ last time and forgot your copy of *Island of the Blue Dolphins.*

6. If the teachers would ___[let]___ me, I would read all day.

7. I ___[left]___ my favorite book on the bus.

8. Will the library ___[let]___ me take out another book?

9. I cannot ___[leave]___ for school before I finish the last chapter.

10. ___[Let]___ me read now, and I will do the dishes later.

Verbs

75

72. Using Forms of Lie and Lay

> The verb *lie* (*lying, lay, has lain*) means "to rest." *Lie* is an intransitive verb and, therefore, cannot have a direct object.
>
> **She <u>lay</u> down for a nap after lunch.**
>
> The verb *lay* (*laying, laid, has laid*) means "to put" or "to place in position." *Lay* is a transitive verb and requires a direct object.
>
> **She <u>laid</u> the vase very carefully on the table.**

A. Circle the correct verb in parentheses.

1. Grandmother often (lay **lies**) down to rest in the afternoon.

2. Today I (lay **laid**) the mail on the table beside the phone.

3. The maid (**laid** lay) the towels on the rack in the bathroom.

4. Pigs were (**lying** laying) in the soft, warm mud.

5. I (laid, **lay**) in the hammock all day yesterday.

6. People often (**lay** lie) flowers on the graves of their loved ones.

7. The children usually (lay **lie**) down for an afternoon nap.

8. (Lie, **Lay**) that box in the corner, please.

9. She had (**lain** laid) awake all night.

10. The pumpkins have (**lain** laid) on the snow-covered field for a week.

B. Complete each sentence with a correct form of *lie* or *lay*. **[Possible answers are given.]**

1. Sand ___[lay]___ on the beach towel.

2. If we ___[lie]___ in the sun too long, we'll burn.

3. We should be ___[lying]___ under the umbrella.

4. The children have ___[laid]___ their sandwiches in the sand.

5. My dog is ___[lying]___ on the sand in the surf.

6. Will you ___[lay]___ the baby on the towel under the umbrella?

7. The bucket and the shovel have ___[lain]___ in the sand all day.

8. She ___[laid]___ the towel too close to the water.

9. She had ___[lain]___ in the sun too much that summer.

10. After applying sunscreen liberally, she ___[laid]___ it next to her.

Verbs

Name_____

73. Using Forms of <u>Sit</u> and <u>Set</u>

> The verb *sit* (*sitting, sat, has sat*) means "to have a place" or "to keep a seat."
>   **He <u>sat</u> there all day, staring into the distance.**
> The verb *set* (*setting, set, has set*) means "to place" or "to fix in position."
>   **She <u>has set</u> the clock for five in the morning.**

A. Circle the correct verb in parentheses.

1. We (sit **set**) the trophy on the top shelf.

2. I (set **sit**) across from my little sister at the dinner table.

3. The dog (**sat** set) all day long on the steps.

4. I (**set** sit) the glass on the table carefully.

5. The hunter will not (sit **set**) a trap for the bear.

6. The children usually (**sit** set) in the back seat of the car.

7. The President has often (set **sat**) at his desk in the Oval Office.

8. Robin, please (sit **set**) the gift under the Christmas tree.

9. My sister always (sets **sits**) too close to the television set.

10. Where shall we (set **sit**)?

B. Complete each sentence with a correct form of *sit* or *set*.

1. Who ____[sat]____ there yesterday?

2. On warm evenings, we ____[sit/sat]____ on the porch.

3. ____[Sit]____ here and rest for a minute.

4. Where shall we ____[set]____ the bookcase?

5. Infants usually ____[sit/sat]____ in high chairs.

6. In school, I ____[sit/sat]____ near the teacher's desk.

7. ____[Set]____ the table for dinner, please.

8. Grandfather always ____[sits/sat]____ in his favorite chair.

9. The nurse ____[sits/sat]____ up all night with the sick child.

10. ____[Set]____ the books on the bottom shelf.

Verbs

77

Name_____

74. Using Forms of Teach and Learn

The verb *teach* (*teaching, taught, has taught*) means "to give instruction" or "to pass knowledge on."

Ana teaches history to fifth graders.

The verb *learn* (*learning, learned, has learned*) means "to receive instruction or knowledge."

I don't know how he learned Spanish in just six months.

A. Circle the correct verb in parentheses.

1. My mother (taught learned) me to cook.

2. I (taught (learned)) to make meatloaf first.

3. Anyone who ((teaches) learns) someone must be patient.

4. My sister (learned (taught)) her husband how to make ravioli.

5. I (taught (learned)) to make that a long time ago.

6. She (learned (taught)) me that cooking is an art.

7. The chef ((teaches) learns) students in his well-equipped kitchen.

8. They (taught (learned)) that they didn't know even the fundamentals of bread making.

9. Mother ((learned) taught) that I like to taste as I go along.

10. I ((taught) learned) myself how to boil an egg.

B. Complete each sentence with a correct form of *teach* or *learn*. **[Possible answers are given.]**

1. What do you _____[teach/learn]_____ at school?

2. They _____[teach/taught]_____ us about math, history, English, and geography.

3. If I am not _____[taught]_____ about Shakespeare, I will be disappointed.

4. We _____[learn/learned]_____ how to divide in fourth grade.

5. The class _____[learns/learned]_____ very slowly.

6. All students have _____[learned]_____ the multiplication facts by sixth grade.

7. In school we _____[learn/learned]_____ how to pronounce difficult words.

8. The teacher _____[teaches/taught]_____ with great patience.

9. She knew we had _____[learned]_____ that last year but thought we should review it.

10. I wish she would _____[teach]_____ us something that was fun to learn.

Verbs

75. Reviewing Verbs

A. Complete the chart with the missing principal parts of the verb. In the last column write whether the verb is regular or irregular.

	PRESENT	PAST	PAST PARTICIPLE	REGULAR OR IRREGULAR
1. break	[breaking]	[broke]	(has) [broken]	[irregular]
2. call	[calling]	[called]	(has) [called]	[regular]
3. like	[liking]	[liked]	(has) [liked]	[regular]
4. choose	[choosing]	[chose]	(has) [chosen]	[irregular]
5. go	[going]	[went]	(has) [gone]	[irregular]

B. Write on the line the tense of the *italicized* verb.

____[past]____ 1. We *walked* along the beach at sunrise.

____[present]____ 2. Rosa *feeds* the pelicans every day.

____[future]____ 3. These tropical flowers *will bloom* in early spring.

__[present progressive]__ 4. Today we *are visiting* the Hawaiian Volcano Observatory.

__[past progressive]__ 5. The jumbo jet *was taxiing* down the runway.

C. Underline the verb phrase in each sentence.

1. Marie had run along the beach.
2. Did you pass by the hot dog stand?
3. Will you take my surfboard to the shore?
4. Scientists can predict where a hurricane will strike the coast.
5. Our team did not win the surfing contest.

D. Circle the correct verb in parentheses.

1. Andrew (broke broken) his new surfboard.
2. We had (see seen) the native ceremony last time.
3. I need to (lie lay) down after snorkeling all day.
4. Please (sit set) the camera carefully on the desk.
5. Joey (lay laid) his sunglasses on the desk.

E. Complete each sentence with the correct verb form.

(Doesn't, Don't) 1 __[Don't]__ forget the story about Bobby and John.

(is, are) 2. At the moment Bobby __[is]__ confused.

(stand, stands) 3. He __[stands]__ wondering who is who.

CONTINUED

Verbs

(smile, smiles)   4. The two boys ___[smile]___ at Bobby.

(Was, Were)   5. ___[Was]___ John the first boy or the second boy?

F.   Write the subject complement in each sentence in the first column. In the second column write whether it is a noun, a pronoun, or an adjective. The linking verb is *italicized*.

1. Perhaps the first boy *was* John.   ___[John]___   ___[noun]___

2. The boys *were* identical.   ___[identical]___   ___[adjective]___

3. Bobby *could be* sleepy.   ___[sleepy]___   ___[adjective]___

4. "It *is* he on my left," Bobby thought.   ___[he]___   ___[pronoun]___

5. "No, he *is* my friend," he thought.   ___[friend]___   ___[noun]___

G.   Write on the line whether the *italicized* verb is transitive or intransitive.

___[intransitive]___   1. Bobby *jumped* in amazement.

___[transitive]___   2. He *grabbed* an arm of each boy.

___[transitive]___   3. He *held* the arms firmly.

___[intransitive]___   4. In a few seconds the boys *laughed* hysterically.

___[intransitive]___   5. They *snickered* to no end.

Try It Yourself
Write four sentences about something funny or amazing that happened to you. Be sure to use verbs correctly.

_____

_____

_____

_____

Check Your Own Work
Choose a selection from your writing portfolio, your journal, a work in progress, an assignment from another class, or a letter. Revise it, applying the skills you have reviewed. The checklist will help you.

✔ Have you used the correct forms of *break, see, go, choose,* and *take?*

✔ Have you used the correct tenses?

✔ Do your subjects agree with your verbs in person and number?

Verbs

Name _____

76. Using Adverbs of Time

> An **adverb** modifies a verb, an adjective, or another adverb.
>
> **He ran swiftly.** (modifies verb *ran*)
> **She is extremely intelligent.** (modifies adjective *intelligent*)
> **My father spoke quite sternly to me.** (modifies adverb *sternly*)
>
> **Adverbs of time** answer the question *when* or *how often*. Some adverbs of time are *again, already, always, before, early, finally, frequently, now, often, soon, today,* and *yesterday*.

A. Underline the adverb in each sentence that tells *when* or *how often*.

1. Kathleen, Mary told me a story yesterday.

2. I had not heard it before.

3. Today she promised to tell me two more.

4. First, an African tale will be presented.

5. Who knows what will happen next!

6. Once there lived a very poor couple.

7. They were usually dressed in rags.

8. They had no children, but they often wished for some.

9. They always hoped for a better future.

10. Sometimes they dreamed about what might happen.

B. Circle the adverb of time in each sentence and write it on the line.

_____[once]_____ 1. The poor man (once) met a man named Abinuku.

_____[soon]_____ 2. They (soon) became friends.

_____[seldom]_____ 3. Abinuku was (seldom) happy or content.

_____[usually]_____ 4. He (usually) held much hate in his heart.

_____[seldom]_____ 5. The poor man (seldom) realized this.

_____[frequently]_____ 6. The poor man (frequently) prayed for a better life.

_____[finally]_____ 7. Help was (finally) promised.

_____[Often]_____ 8. (Often) Money, Child, and Patience would visit him.

_____[then]_____ 9. He would (then) have to choose which to keep.

_____[ever]_____ 10. How could he (ever) choose?

77. Using Adverbs of Place

> **Adverbs of place** answer the question *where*.
>
> **The farmer fell <u>backward</u> into the haystack.**
> (Where did the farmer fall? Backward)
>
> Some adverbs of place are *above, away, backward, below, down, forth, here, in, out, there,* and *up*.

A. Underline the adverb in each sentence that tells *where*.

1. We stood <u>there</u> on the busiest corner.

2. My mother shops <u>here</u>.

3. We looked <u>upward</u> to the top of the new mall.

4. Someone decided it was time to go <u>forward</u> and shop.

5. I would go <u>in</u> if I had money.

6. She took the escalator <u>down</u> to the floor with the shoe stores.

7. The salesperson walked <u>away</u> from the store.

8. Her friend walked <u>on</u> as she sampled the perfume.

9. They all met <u>inside</u> to have lunch.

10. I walked <u>ahead</u> toward the dress of my dreams.

B. Complete each sentence with an adverb of place. **[Possible answers are given.]**

1. You will find the athletes _____[inside]_____, near the locker room.

2. They won't come _____[out]_____ before they stretch.

3. Their fans congregate _____[everywhere]_____.

4. They like playing tennis _____[here]_____ at Wimbledon.

5. Finally they walked _____[down]_____ toward the court.

6. The judges came _____[forward]_____ and greeted them, wishing them both luck.

7. A line judge stood _____[there]_____, staring at the line.

8. The player ran _____[up]_____ to the net.

9. The camera crew moved _____[backward]_____ when the player approached them.

10. The winner walked _____[away]_____ from the match with a trophy and a smile.

78. Using Adverbs of Manner

> **Adverbs of manner** answer the question *how*.
>
> **The contestant spelled the word <u>correctly</u>.**
> (How did the contestant spell the word? Correctly)
>
> Some adverbs of manner are *carefully, correctly, fast, gracefully, hard, kindly, quickly, softly, swiftly, truthfully,* and *well.*

A. Underline the adverb in each sentence that tells *how* or *in what manner.*

1. The court jester danced <u>wildly</u> for the king.

2. Queen Jane wore her crown <u>beautifully</u>.

3. The serfs worked <u>diligently</u> in the fields.

4. They suffered <u>greatly</u> from their poor living conditions.

5. The king spoke <u>distinctly</u> to his subjects.

6. Two guards stood <u>silently</u> at the castle's gate.

7. They <u>proudly</u> protected the castle.

8. The guard <u>carefully</u> aimed his bow and arrow.

9. The king's army fought <u>heroically</u> at the Battle of York.

10. The king and queen danced <u>elegantly</u> at the ball.

Adverbs

B. Complete each sentence with an adverb of manner.

1. Joshua draws and paints _____[well]_____.

2. He applies the paint very _____[carefully]_____.

3. His hand draws _____[steadily]_____ on the paper.

4. No one speaks _____[loudly]_____ in his studio.

5. I come to see his art _____[eagerly]_____.

6. When I paint, I move the brush _____[lazily]_____.

7. I must go to art class _____[quickly]_____.   **[Possible answers are given.]**

8. In class we paint and draw _____[happily]_____.

9. Josh likes to draw when music is playing _____[softly]_____.

10. He paints _____[diligently]_____ every morning.

79. Reviewing Adverbs of Time, Place, and Manner

Underline the adverb in each sentence.
Write on the line whether it expresses time, place, or manner.

__[manner]__ 1. In Omaha, Nebraska, Father Edward J. Flanagan <u>regularly</u> studied the plight of young boys who were orphans, delinquents, and criminals.

__[time]__ 2. He decided to work <u>daily</u> for their cause.

__[place]__ 3. For the boys to move <u>forward</u> in life, they needed an education.

__[time]__ 4. Father Flanagan started what is <u>now</u> the Girls and Boys Town school system.

__[manner]__ 5. He <u>earnestly</u> collected money to rent an old mansion as a home for boys.

__[place]__ 6. Father Flanagan's policy was to welcome any boy who wanted to be <u>there</u>.

__[time]__ 7. The boys played sports and <u>frequently</u> played music.

__[manner]__ 8. When the school outgrew that space, Father Flanagan <u>determinedly</u> found another.

__[place]__ 9. Father Flanagan bought a farm that was situated <u>nearby</u>.

__[time]__ 10. A home could <u>finally</u> be built to accommodate all the boys.

__[manner]__ 11. On it the boys could work <u>hard</u> and produce some of their own food.

__[time]__ 12. This home would <u>soon</u> be called Boys Town.

__[place]__ 13. Girls and Boys Towns can be found <u>everywhere</u> throughout the country.

__[manner]__ 14. Their workers <u>tirelessly</u> serve not only girls and boys but families as well.

__[manner]__ 15. We need people like Father Flanagan, who have faith in humanity and who give <u>generously</u> of themselves.

Father Flanagan cared for boys who were outcasts of society. He believed in them when no one else did. Give an example of something kind you can do for someone in your class or school who is not accepted by the crowd.

80. Comparing with Adverbs

Many adverbs have three **degrees of comparison**: positive, comparative, and superlative.

The comparative of most adverbs that end in *-ly* is formed by adding *more* or *less* before the positive.

The superlative is formed by adding *most* or *least* before the positive.

quickly	more quickly	most quickly
sadly	less sadly	least sadly

The comparative of adverbs that don't end in *-ly* is formed by adding *-er*.

The superlative is formed by adding *-est*.

soon	sooner	soonest
far	farther	farthest

A. Underline the adverb in each sentence.
Write on the line the degree of comparison.

_____[positive]_____ 1. The rooster woke us <u>early</u> in the morning.

_____[comparative]_____ 2. A cheetah can run <u>faster</u> than a lion.

_____[superlative]_____ 3. The brown puppy opened its eyes <u>widest</u> of all.

_____[comparative]_____ 4. In the city you will see squirrels <u>more often</u> than rabbits.

_____[positive]_____ 5. The old man treats his cats <u>kindly</u>.

_____[positive]_____ 6. The beaver worked <u>hard</u> at building the dam.

_____[comparative]_____ 7. The seagull flew <u>higher</u> than the pelican.

_____[positive]_____ 8. The bear cub tried <u>earnestly</u> to catch a salmon.

_____[comparative]_____ 9. A snail travels <u>slower</u> than many other animals.

_____[superlative]_____ 10. Of all the animals, I think the gazelle runs the <u>most gracefully</u>.

B. Circle the correct adverb in parentheses.

1. Of all the rainy days, it is raining (harder (**hardest**)) today.

2. You must walk (carefully (**more carefully**)) when it is raining than when it is not.

3. We ((**politely**) more politely) folded our umbrellas when we entered her house.

4. The eagle flew (high (**higher**)) than the clouds to avoid the rain.

5. This is the (more awful (**most awful**)) weather we've had in a long time.

Adverbs

81. Using Good and Well

> The word *good* is an adjective. Adjectives modify nouns or pronouns.
> *Good* may follow a linking verb as a subject complement.
>
> **The delicious pizza was a good choice.** (modifies the noun *choice*)
> **They are good at playing soccer.** (modifies the pronoun *they*)
>
> *Good* answers the question *what kind*.
>
> **She was a good babysitter.**
> (*What kind* of babysitter was she? Good)
>
> The word *well* is generally an adverb. Adverbs usually modify verbs.
> *Well* modifies a verb and answers the question *how*.
>
> **Susan plays well with other children.**
> (*How* does she play with other children? Well)

A. Circle the correct word in parentheses.

1. Andy cleaned his room (good (well)).
2. Every room could use a ((good) well) dusting.
3. ((Good) Well) cleaning supplies will help a lot.
4. If you don't wipe the window (good (well)), it will have streaks.
5. Lots of ((good) well) elbow grease is what we need.
6. Did you know that newspaper dries a mirror or window (good (well))?
7. It's a ((good) well) thing that we have the whole day to finish cleaning.
8. If we don't do a ((good) well) job, your mother will notice.
9. He doesn't do as (good (well)) with the broom and mop as he does with the vacuum cleaner.
10. We have worked together (good (well)) and now have an immaculate house.

B. Complete each sentence with *good* or *well*.

1. The shining sun seemed to say it was going to be a __[good]__ day.
2. For some reason I couldn't listen __[well]__ in class today.
3. I had no __[good]__ reason for misspelling that easy word.
4. The teacher explained the decimal problem __[well]__.
5. When things don't go __[well]__, I consult my older brother.

Adverbs

82. Using Their and There

> *Their* is an adjective that shows possession or ownership.
> It is followed by the noun it modifies.
>
> **Their house was so big we couldn't believe it.**
>
> *There* is an adverb and means "in that place."
> *There* is sometimes used as an introductory word.
>
> **I placed the presents on the table over <u>there</u>.**
> **<u>There</u> are so many people here, will we ever find a seat?**

A. Complete each sentence with *their* or *there*.

1. The arboretum has so many beautiful trees and shrubs
   that the Pecks go ___[there]___ every fall.

2. Many of the trees shed ___[their]___ leaves each year.

3. The sugar maples over ___[there]___ have started to turn color.

4. ___[There]___ must be a hundred different shades of yellow and red.

5. Mrs. Peck's favorite tree is the orange and red one over ___[there]___.

6. ___[There]___ are so many beautiful trees in this clearing.

7. ___[Their]___ Christmas picture was taken among such trees last fall.

8. Is that ___[their]___ little girl climbing the tree?

9. You can't play soccer or football on the grass ___[there]___, though.

10. ___[Their]___ guess was that this rule helped to keep the arboretum's
    grass, trees, and shrubs from harm.

B. Circle the correct word in parentheses.

1. The campers cooked ((their) there) breakfast on the open fire.

2. They pitched ((their) there) tents over by the trees.

3. They heard a noise over (their (there)) in the bushes.

4. ((Their) there) hair stood up on end.

5. What if a bear was waiting (their (there)) for them?

6. They decided (their (there)) was nothing they could do.

7. (Their (There)) was the trailhead.

8. They had brought ((their) there) rain gear just in case the weather turned foul.

9. (Their (There)) on the tree, almost obscured by the thick leaves, was the trail marker.

10. The highlight of ((their) there) day was standing at the end of the trail
    looking out over the valley.

83. Using <u>Real</u> and <u>Very</u>

> *Real* is an adjective and means "genuine or true."
> **As hard as it is to believe, that was a <u>real</u> diamond on her finger.**
>
> *Very* is an adverb and means "extremely or to a high degree."
> **Marina was <u>very</u> cautious as she walked along the ledge.**

A. Complete each sentence with *real* or *very*.

1. I am always ___[very]___ happy to visit the art museum.

2. You can see many ___[real]___ masterpieces there.

3. They were ___[very]___ eager to see Edgar Degas's work.

4. Degas sculpted ballerinas and other women ___[very]___ well.

5. Degas used ___[real]___ ballerinas as models.

6. He was ___[very]___ interested in capturing the mood of the dancers backstage.

7. The art student had a ___[real]___ interest in art depicting dance.

8. The museum shop has a ___[very]___ good collection of Degas reproductions.

9. Of course, we'd all rather have the ___[real]___ thing.

10. It was ___[very]___ thoughtful of you to buy me this tiny Degas dancer.

B. Circle the correct word in parentheses.

1. Brioche is a (real ⟨very⟩) tasty kind of bread.

2. It is made with lots of (⟨real⟩ very) butter.

3. When I am (real ⟨very⟩) hungry, a brioche and some tea are the perfect snack.

4. I am (real ⟨very⟩) picky about the breads I eat.

5. They must be (real ⟨very⟩) fresh.

6. The (⟨real⟩ very) recipe for that bread can be found in Mother's cookbook.

7. Fresh bread is a gift of (⟨real⟩ very) appeal for many people.

8. The crust is (real ⟨very⟩) brown and crunchy.

9. The (⟨real⟩ very) test of a good bread is if Grandma will eat it.

10. Thick slices of fresh bread help make for a (real ⟨very⟩) good sandwich.

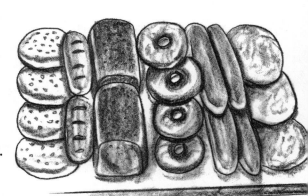

84. Using <u>To</u>, <u>Too</u>, and <u>Two</u>

> *To* is a preposition. It is usually used to indicate motion toward some place, person, or thing.
>
> **Let's go <u>to</u> the store.**
>
> *Too* is an adverb and means "also, more than enough, or besides."
>
> **Are you coming along <u>too</u>?**
>
> *Two* is a noun or an adjective and refers to the number 2.
>
> **The <u>two</u> actresses shared the award.**

A. Complete each sentence with *to*, *too*, or *two*.

1. In the United States there are __[two]__ major mountain ranges.

2. Some of the mountains were __[too]__ high for the pioneers to cross with their wagons.

3. Have you ever gone __[to]__ Colorado and seen the Rocky Mountains?

4. The __[two]__ of you should go and see them someday.

5. I wonder if they would be __[too]__ difficult to climb.

6. It would take more than __[two]__ days to reach the summit.

7. I could never take __[too]__ many pictures of those gorgeous snow-covered peaks.

8. They went __[to]__ the gym that has the climbing wall.

9. __[Two]__ months of practice should get them ready for their climb.

10. Finally they put on their packs and started their trek __[to]__ to the mountains.

B. Circle the correct word in parentheses.

1. I like carrots, but I like spinach (two (too) to).

2. The farmer must take his vegetables (two too (to)) market.

3. Are there ((two) too to) ripe eggplants in that basket?

4. I think I bought (two (too) to) many squashes.

5. I prefer the outdoor farmers' market (two too (to)) the supermarket.

6. We'll have ((two) too to) kinds of beans for dinner tonight.

7. If you eat (two (too) to) many carrots, you'll turn orange.

8. Can you name ((two) too to) kinds of lettuce?

9. Brussels sprouts and turnips are ((two) too to) of my least favorite vegetables.

10. The corn was sent off (two too (to)) many stores in the area.

Adverbs

85. Using No, Not, and Never

> A negative idea is expressed by using one negative word.
> This negative word may be *no, not, none, never,* or *nothing.*
>
> **There was <u>nothing</u> she could say to make me change my mind.**
>
> These words should be used only when there are no other
> negative words in sentences.

A. Circle the correct word in parentheses.

1. None of my friends has (ever never) seen a farm.

2. Aren't there (any no) farms near the city?

3. I have (ever never) ridden on a tractor.

4. There were (any no) scarecrows in the fields.

5. Didn't she gather (any no) eggs from the hens?

6. Isn't there (anything nothing) I can do for the harvest?

7. Haven't you baled (any no) hay?

8. There are (any no) farmhands on this farm at all.

9. There was (any no) way to save the crop.

10. She has (ever never) even held a pitchfork.

B. Complete each sentence to express a negative idea.

1. Bill hasn't ___[any]___ mail in his mailbox.

2. Haven't you ___[ever]___ received a package by special delivery?

3. I have ___[never/not]___ been sent flowers.

4. Didn't you bring ___[any]___ stamps with you?

5. This package hasn't ___[any]___ postage.

6. There was ___[no]___ address on this envelope.

7. Vince has ___[never/not]___ had a pen pal.

8. You can't write if you haven't ___[any]___ stationery.

9. Haven't you ___[ever]___ received a chain letter?

10. Aren't there ___[any]___ mailboxes nearby?

Adverbs

86. Reviewing Adverbs

A. Write on the line whether the *italicized* adverb is an adverb of time, place, or manner.

_____[time]_____ 1. A storm hit our town *yesterday*.

_____[manner]_____ 2. We *hurriedly* ran inside our house.

_____[manner]_____ 3. My family had prepared *well* for storms.

_____[manner]_____ 4. We looked *excitedly* out the window.

_____[manner]_____ 5. The sky got dark *quickly*.

_____[time]_____ 6. The wind gusted *next*.

_____[place]_____ 7. The garbage can lid was blown *high*.

_____[place]_____ 8. Our neighbor's lawn chair blew *away*.

_____[place]_____ 9. After being tossed by the wind, the mailbox crashed *down*.

_____[time]_____ 10. *Finally*, the storm was over!

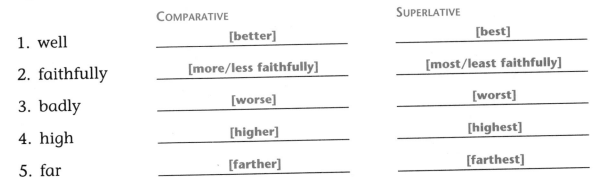

Adverbs

B. Complete each chart with the comparative and superlative degree of each adverb.

	COMPARATIVE	SUPERLATIVE
1. well	[better]	[best]
2. faithfully	[more/less faithfully]	[most/least faithfully]
3. badly	[worse]	[worst]
4. high	[higher]	[highest]
5. far	[farther]	[farthest]

C. Write **P** on the line if the *italicized* adverb is positive, **C** if it is comparative degree, or **S** if it is superlative degree.

__[C]__ 1. Scott is feeling *better* today.

__[P]__ 2. The ship glided *smoothly* over the water.

__[S]__ 3. Gretchen swam *best* of all the swimmers.

__[P]__ 4. My dog *faithfully* brings me the paper from the porch.

__[C]__ 5. I study *more diligently* for science tests than for social studies tests.

CONTINUED

D. Circle the correct word in parentheses.

1. The poor man went (**to** two too) Abinuku to ask his advice.

2. Abinuku was (**very** real) jealous of him.

3. Abinuku (ever **never**) wanted the poor man to be happy.

4. "You must choose (good **well**)," Abinuku said.

5. "(**There** Their) should be careful thought," he said.

6. "A (**good** well) choice," he said, "would be Patience."

7. Abinuku thought, "It won't bring him (no **any**) happiness."

8. The poor man rejected the other (to **two** too) choices.

9. At first his wife was (**very** real) angry.

10. Eventually, however, Patience brought them (very **real**) joy.

11. They became more content with (there **their**) lives.

12. They couldn't remember (**ever** never) being so happy.

13. In time Money and Child came to them (to two **too**).

14. (There **Their**) joy was complete!

15. In the end, Abinuku had advised the poor man (good **well**).

Try It Yourself
Write four sentences about a storm or other severe weather
you have witnessed. Be sure to use adverbs correctly.

_____

_____

_____

_____

Check Your Own Work
Choose a selection from your writing portfolio, your journal,
a work in progress, an assignment from another class, or a letter.
Revise it, applying the skills you have reviewed.
The checklist will help you.

✔ Have you included appropriate adverbs of time, place, and manner?

✔ Have you used the correct degree of comparison for the adverbs?

✔ Have you used *good* and *well*, *their* and *there*, and *real* and *very* correctly?

Name _____

87. Recognizing Prepositions and Prepositional Phrases

> A **preposition** is a word that relates a noun or a pronoun to some other word in the sentence. The noun or pronoun that follows the preposition is the object of the preposition.
>
> > **Little Red Riding Hood went <u>into</u> the woods.**
> > (*Woods* is the object of the preposition *into*.)
>
> A preposition and the noun or pronoun that follows it are separate words, but they do the work of a single modifier. This group of related words is called a phrase. Because it is introduced by a preposition, it is called a **prepositional phrase**.
>
> > **Little Red Riding Hood went <u>into the woods</u>.**
>
> Here are some common prepositions.
>
> | | | | | | |
> |---|---|---|---|---|---|
> | about | against | between | for | of | to |
> | above | among | by | from | off | toward |
> | across | at | down | in | on | under |
> | after | before | during | into | over | up |
> | around | beside | except | near | through | with |

A. Circle the prepositions in these sentences.

1. John Chapman was born (in) Massachusetts (in) 1775.
2. He had a great love (for) apples.
3. Johnny's dream was planting apple trees (in) the West.
4. His dream could not come true (without) seeds.
5. He went (into) several orchards and collected a lot (of) seeds.

B. Circle the preposition(s) and underline the prepositional phrase(s) in each sentence.

1. (At) first, he gave bags (of) seeds (to) settlers.
2. Later he traveled (to) Pennsylvania.
3. (After) some time, he journeyed (to) the Ohio Valley.
4. Johnny took apple seeds (with) him everywhere.
5. He planted them (beside) running streams.
6. He also planted them (on) rolling hills.
7. He could not notice a fertile area (without) stopping.
8. Johnny moved (from) place (to) place, planting more seeds.
9. (Throughout) the area he became known (as) Johnny Appleseed.
10. Thanks (to) him, the Ohio Valley is rich (in) apple trees.

88. Writing Prepositions

A. Complete each sentence with an appropriate preposition.
[Possible answers are given.]

1. We enjoyed ourselves sledding _____[on]_____ the hill.

2. James slid _____[into]_____ a snow bank.

3. Don't fall _____[off]_____ the sled, James.

4. Vince took the ski lift _____[up]_____ the mountain.

5. He skied _____[down]_____ the slopes.

6. We took a sleigh ride _____[through]_____ the woods.

7. The ride took us _____[toward]_____ a stream.

8. We went _____[over]_____ a snow-covered bridge.

9. Ice skate _____[with]_____ us, Anna.

10. Her skates were a gift _____[from]_____ her aunt.

11. They skated _____[at]_____ the park.

12. Carl went ice fishing _____[with]_____ his father.

13. They fished _____[on]_____ Lake Winnemac.

14. They kept warm _____[inside]_____ the little house.

15. We drank hot chocolate _____[near]_____ the fire.

B. Complete each sentence with a prepositional phrase. [Answers will vary.]

1. The gardener bent _____.

2. He planted the wildflower seeds _____.

3. He put some fertilizer _____.

4. I gave the gardener a spade, which he placed _____.

5. The gardener placed a bouquet _____.

89. Using <u>Between</u> and <u>Among</u>

Use *between* when speaking of two persons, places, or things.
Let's keep this information <u>between</u> you and me.

Use *among* when speaking of more than two persons, places, or things.
The singer stood unrecognized <u>among</u> her fans.

A. Circle the correct preposition in parentheses.

1. Amy walked (between among) her two sisters.
2. The United States lies (between among) the Atlantic and Pacific Oceans.
3. Distribute the papers (between among) the students in the class.
4. A beautiful flower grew (between among) the weeds.
5. The band marched (between among) two lines of spectators.
6. The two boys carried the injured man (between among) them.
7. A lasting friendship exists (between among) the United States and Canada.
8. Is that a secret (between among) the two of you?
9. Our airplane is (between among) those on the runway.
10. You may sit (between among) Austin and me.
11. Alabama is (between among) Georgia and Mississippi.
12. Our leaders work for peace (between among) all the nations of the world.
13. Share the fruit (between among) the four of you.
14. The flower arrangement sat (between among) two candles.
15. Not one (between among) the students would volunteer to go first.

B. Complete each sentence with *between* or *among*.

1. Those five boys often quarrel _____[among]_____ themselves.
2. Trade is carried on _____[between]_____ North and South America.
3. There isn't one tall player _____[among]_____ the five.
4. _____[Between]_____ you and me, whom shall we choose?
5. The awards were divided _____[among]_____ the three top winners.
6. There is a joyful spirit _____[among]_____ the students in our class.
7. The garage stands _____[between]_____ the house and the barn.
8. There was one stranger _____[among]_____ the four visitors.
9. _____[Between]_____ them, the two brothers made the model ship.
10. May I walk _____[between]_____ Ian and you?

Name_____

90. Using From and Off

> Use *from* when speaking of a person from whom something is received.
> **The invitation was <u>from</u> my neighbors.**
>
> Use *off* to mean "away from." The expression *off of* is never correct.
> **The pitcher fell <u>off</u> the table.**

A. Circle the correct preposition in parentheses.

1. Be careful or you will fall (from (off)) that chair.
2. When you enter the room, take your hat (from (off)).
3. We bought corn ((from) off) the farmer.
4. She swept the leaves (off of (off)) the porch.
5. ((From) Off) whom did you receive that interesting book?
6. Take the message ((from) off) him, please.
7. Who slid (off of (off)) the seat?
8. Her pen rolled (from (off)) her desk onto the floor.
9. These skates are a gift ((from) off) my uncle.
10. My mother requested some books ((from) off) the librarian.
11. The boy hopped (from (off)) his bicycle.
12. This watch is a present ((from) off) my grandparents.
13. The puppy knocked the decorations (from (off)) the tree.
14. It was hard to get the top (off of (off)) the ketchup bottle.
15. This sourdough bread is (off (from)) the corner bakery.

B. Complete each sentence with *from* or *off*.

1. Don't jump ___[off]___ the step.
2. We get peanuts ___[from]___ farmers.
3. The farmhand hopped ___[off]___ the tractor.
4. My mother buys delicious cakes ___[from]___ that baker.
5. I get interesting books ___[from]___ my uncle.
6. The sign read, "Keep ___[off]___ the grass."
7. The lid fell ___[off]___ the tin can.
8. Kevin stepped ___[off]___ the train quickly.
9. I learned how to print ___[from]___ my teacher.
10. You may get a paper ___[from]___ the instructor.

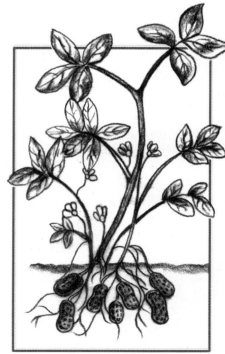

(sidebar) **Prepositions, Conjunctions, Interjections**

91. Recognizing Adjectival Phrases

> An **adjectival phrase** is a prepositional phrase used as an adjective.
> Adjectival phrases contain a preposition and an object.
> **The ballerina <u>with the pink tutu</u> danced gracefully.**

A. Underline the adjectival phrase in each sentence. Identify the noun each adjectival phrase modifies. Write the noun on the line.

__[flowers]__ 1. The flowers <u>in the vase</u> look lovely.

__[garden]__ 2. They are from the garden <u>behind the house</u>.

__[roses]__ 3. The roses <u>along the trellis</u> are red, yellow, and pink.

__[ivy]__ 4. The ivy <u>on the house</u> is growing quickly.

__[tree]__ 5. The tree <u>beside the house</u> shades the lawn.

__[daffodils]__ 6. The daffodils <u>with their bright yellow trumpets</u> stand nearby.

__[zinnias]__ 7. The zinnias <u>near the trellis</u> are very cheerful.

__[bush]__ 8. The lilac bush <u>in the corner</u> is fragrant and colorful.

__[lilies]__ 9. The lilies <u>in this garden</u> have very showy flowers.

__[bush]__ 10. The bush <u>with the heart-shaped flowers</u> is called a bleeding heart.

B. Read the paragraph. Underline the adjectival phrases. Circle the noun each phrase modifies.

Are you a (person) <u>with hay fever</u>? Hay fever is an (allergy) <u>with definite symptoms</u>. All (seasons) <u>except winter</u> are bad (times) <u>for sufferers</u>. This allergy produces uncomfortable (irritations) <u>in the eyes, nose, and throat</u>. The (eyes) <u>of the victim</u> may become red, itchy, and watery. The (nose) <u>with its swollen membranes</u> may itch and run. The (throat) <u>with its sensitivity</u> becomes irritated. "What is the (cause) <u>of all this grief</u>?" you ask. (Pollen) <u>from plants</u> is the culprit! If you have (symptoms) <u>of this annoying condition</u>, seek help. Your doctor can supply a remedy.

Prepositions, Conjunctions, Interjections

92. Writing Adjectival Phrases

Rewrite each sentence, changing the *italicized* adjective to an adjectival phrase. **[Possible answers are given.]**

1. The *tour* guide spoke perfect English.

   [The guide of the tour spoke perfect English.]

2. She pointed out the *marble* statue.

   [She pointed out the statue of marble.]

3. Then she showed us the *da Vinci* painting.

   [Then she showed us the painting by da Vinci.]

4. The *gold* crown was behind glass.

   [The crown of gold was behind glass.]

5. But we could touch the *silver* rings.

   [But we could touch the rings of silver.]

6. The *American* tourist asked many questions.

   [The tourist from America asked many questions.]

7. His wife wanted to stop for some *Italian* coffee.

   [His wife wanted to stop for some coffee from Italy.]

8. We were all hoping there would be some *French* bread.

   [We were all hoping there would be some bread from France.]

9. We settled for *cheese* sandwiches.

   [We settled for sandwiches of cheese.]

10. The *tour* bus could not fit between the cars.

    [The bus for the tour could not fit between the cars.]

Name_____

93. Recognizing Adverbial Phrases

> An **adverbial phrase** is a prepositional phrase used as an adverb.
> Adverbial phrases contain a preposition and an object.
> **The rain drove the team into the dugout.**

A. Underline the adverbial phrase in each sentence.
Write on the line the verb it modifies.

_____[look]_____ 1. The tour guide asked the group to look into the past.

_____[jousted]_____ 2. She described the knights who jousted outside the castle walls.

_____[watched]_____ 3. The lord of the castle watched from the battlements.

_____[sat]_____ 4. His lady sat in the keep, or great tower.

_____[lowered]_____ 5. The guards lowered the drawbridge over the moat.

_____[stood]_____ 6. When drawn, the bridge stood against the gate.

_____[shot]_____ 7. The guards shot through the loopholes in the castle walls.

_____[feasted]_____ 8. All the castle's residents feasted in the great hall.

_____[disappeared]_____ 9. The lady disappeared up the spiral staircase.

_____[came]_____ 10. The feast's herbs and vegetables came from the castle's small garden.

B. Complete each sentence with an adverbial phrase. **[Possible answers are given.]**

1. The plane flies _____[over the ocean.]_____

2. We traveled _____[to foreign lands.]_____

3. We gave our passports _____[to the customs official.]_____

4. The porter placed our bags _____[on the cart.]_____

5. The pickpocket reached _____[into my bag.]_____

6. We bought the strange fruit _____[in the market.]_____

7. I put the train tickets _____[on the counter.]_____

8. My passport fell _____[out of the pouch.]_____

9. The peddler grabbed the money _____[from my hand.]_____

10. We won't travel again _____[without travelers' checks.]_____

Prepositions, Conjunctions, Interjections

99

Name_____

94. Writing Adverbial Phrases

Rewrite each sentence, changing the *italicized* adverb
to an adverbial phrase. [Possible answers are given.]

1. The surgeon operated *skillfully* on the patient.

   [The surgeon operated with skill on the patient.]

2. The patient lay *silently* on the operating table.

   [The patient lay in silence on the operating table.]

3. Her husband paced *worriedly* up and down the hallway.

   [Her husband paced with worry up and down the hallway.]

4. The patient recovered *speedily*.

   [The patient recovered with speed.]

5. The bandages were changed *gently* by the nurse.

   [The bandages were changed with gentleness by the nurse.]

6. The night nurse ran the floor *efficiently*.

   [The night nurse ran the floor with efficiency.]

7. The technician drew the blood *quickly*.

   [The technician drew the blood with quickness.]

8. The elderly patient moved her leg *painfully*.

   [The elderly patient moved her leg with pain.]

9. The orderly pushed the gurney *clumsily* into the elevator.

   [The orderly pushed the gurney with clumsiness into the elevator.]

10. The doctor diagnosed the problem *expertly*.

    [The doctor diagnosed the problem with expertise.]

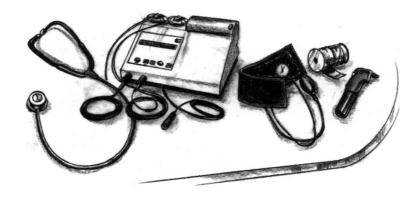

Name_____

95. Distinguishing Between Adjectival and Adverbial Phrases

Read the sentences. Circle the adjectival phrases.
Underline the adverbial phrases.

1. The Statue of Liberty stands in New York Harbor.

2. It was erected in 1886.

3. It was a gift from France.

4. "Liberty Enlightening the World" was the name the French gave to the statue.

5. "The New Colossus" was another name given to the statue.

6. This title comes from a poem.

7. The poem was written by Emma Lazarus.

8. She was a poet from New York City.

9. She called the statue "Mother of Exiles" in her poem.

10. The statue in the poem gives a "world-wide welcome."

11. What she stated in her poem was true.

12. In the late 1800s America was welcoming many immigrants.

13. These were immigrants from the whole world.

14. Emma cared particularly about the Jewish people who came here, because she herself was Jewish.

15. Her family could trace its Jewish heritage to America's early settlement.

16. She spoke on Jewish issues.

17. She started classes for Jewish immigrants.

18. She helped them find housing in the city.

19. She published her poem "The New Colossus" in 1883.

20. Her poem eventually was printed on the Statue of Liberty's plaque.

Emma Lazarus tried to help people who were new to this country. Give an example of something you can do to help someone who is new to your class, school, or neighborhood.

96. Using Conjunctions to Connect Subjects

A **conjunction** connects words or groups of words.
The most common conjunctions are *and*, *or*, and *but*.

> **Would you like the cookie <u>or</u> the muffin?**
> **Cake <u>and</u> ice cream are usually served at birthday parties.**
> **He brought me not a hot piece of pizza <u>but</u> a cold, soggy sandwich.**

The parts of a compound subject are connected by a conjunction.

> **Green eggs <u>and</u> ham were the subject of a children's book.**

A. Circle the conjunction in each sentence. Underline the subjects it connects.

1. <u>Yesterday</u> (and) <u>today</u> were special program days at my school.
2. The <u>students</u> (or) the <u>teachers</u> are going to sit in the front rows.
3. <u>Tracy</u> (and) <u>Trina</u> sat next to each other on the bleachers.
4. The <u>cheerleaders</u> (or) <u>basketball players</u> will act as ushers.
5. <u>Singing</u> (and) <u>dancing</u> were going to go on today.
6. The <u>band</u> (and) the <u>bandleader</u> were practicing.
7. A <u>singer</u> (or) a <u>dancer</u> will be the featured attraction.
8. <u>Talk</u> (and) <u>laughter</u> filled the gym.
9. The lead <u>singer</u> (and) the <u>chorus</u> sang soulfully.
10. The <u>music</u> (and) <u>dance</u> mesmerized the audience.

B. Complete each sentence with a conjunction to connect the subjects. [Possible answers are given.]

1. Elizabeth __[and]__ Tina study together.
2. He __[and/or]__ I will borrow the class notes.
3. The teacher __[and/or]__ the aide will administer the test.
4. Not you __[but]__ I am unprepared for this test.
5. The test __[and]__ an answer grid were placed on my desk.

C. Complete each sentence with a compound subject. [Possible answers are given.]

1. __[Adults]__ and __[children]__ like picnics.
2. __[Blankets]__ and __[baskets]__ were placed on the ground.
3. Not __[Terrence]__ but __[Jonas]__ brought the grill.
4. __[Ketchup]__ or __[mustard]__ goes on my hotdog, but not both.
5. Not __[dancing]__ but __[singing]__ goes on all afternoon.

97. Using Conjunctions to Connect Predicates

> The verbs in a compound predicate are connected by a conjunction.
> **The picnickers talked _and_ ate all afternoon.**

A. Circle the conjunction in each sentence.
Underline the verbs it connects.

1. I awakened (and) slid out of bed.

2. I washed (and) dried my face.

3. For breakfast I toast some bread
   (or) fix cereal with fruit.

4. I put on my hat (and) slipped on my gloves.

5. I take my backpack (but) often carry my lunch.

6. I waved (and) yelled to get the bus driver's attention.

7. My friends talk (or) sing on the bus.

8. We were tested (and) quizzed many times on the Constitution.

9. I usually walked (but) sometimes ran to the bus stop.

10. The teacher listened (and) commented thoughtfully each time I talked.

B. Complete each sentence. Use a conjunction to connect the verbs.

1. The baby cried __[and]__ laughed at different times today.

2. The mother hugged __[and]__ kissed the baby.

3. The father did not feed __[but]__ washed the baby.

4. The baby cannot walk __[and/or]__ talk yet.

5. The baby's cereal heats __[and]__ bubbles very quickly.

C. Complete each sentence with a compound predicate. **[Possible answers are given.]**

1. The old car ____[rumbles]____ and ____[creaks]____.

2. We ____[washed]____ and ____[waxed]____ it.

3. Afterward it ____[glistened]____ and ____[shone]____ in the sun.

4. We ____[called]____ and ____[waved]____ to our friends
   as we drove it through town.

5. It ____[spat]____ and ____[sputtered]____ when we changed gears.

98. Using Conjunctions to Connect Direct Objects

> The parts of a compound direct object are connected by a conjunction.
> **The carpenter carried a hammer <u>and</u> a saw.**

A. Circle the conjunction in each sentence. Underline the direct objects it connects.

1. Airplanes transport <u>mail</u> (and) <u>passengers</u>.

2. Many passengers dislike not <u>takeoff</u> (but) <u>landing</u>.

3. Flight attendants bring <u>food</u> (and) <u>drinks</u> to passengers.

4. They usually offer <u>beef</u> (or) <u>chicken</u>.

5. Passengers often have <u>cell phones</u> (and) <u>laptop computers</u>.

6. A flight attendant explains <u>safety precautions</u> (and) <u>flight rules</u>.

7. She also mentions <u>seat belts</u> (and) <u>floatation devices</u>.

8. Often a flight attendant must practice <u>patience</u> (and) <u>kindness</u> with a troublesome passenger.

9. The pilot shares with the passengers the plane's current <u>location</u> (and) its estimated <u>time</u> of arrival.

10. Flight attendants provide not <u>entertainment</u> (but) <u>safety</u>.

B. Complete each sentence. Use a conjunction to connect the direct objects.

1. The model was wearing a fur coat __[and]__ a hat.

2. She applied foundation __[and]__ blush to her face.

3. Her agent didn't like her makeup [and/or] her clothes.

4. The photographer scrutinized the shadows __[and]__ light on the model's face.

5. The model offered not frowns __[but]__ smiles to the camera.

C. Complete each sentence with a compound direct object. **[Possible answers are given.]**

1. For a first course we were offered not ____[salad]____ but ____[soup]____.

2. The waiter served ____[pie]____ and ____[cake]____ for dessert.

3. We got our ____[coats]____ and ____[hats]____ from the coat check.

4. We would take a ____[bus]____ or a ____[taxi]____ home.

5. We would watch ____[TV]____ or a ____[video]____ once we got home.

Name_____

99. Using Conjunctions to Connect Sentences

> Sentences can be connected by a conjunction.
>
> **I kept the sturdy raincoat, <u>but</u> I returned the flimsy jacket.**

A. Read the two sentences in each example. Add a conjunction to connect the two sentences. Use *and*, *but*, or *or*. In some cases, more than one conjunction may be correct.

1. Diamonds are precious gems, __[but]__ they are also used for industry.

2. You can wear diamonds on your fingers, __[and]__ you can use diamonds to cut glass.

3. The diamond was insured, __[but]__ she was still afraid to wear it.

4. You must clean and polish your diamond ring, __[or]__ it will look dull.

5. A cubic zirconium looks like a real diamond, __[but]__ it doesn't cost as much as a real diamond.

6. The diamond is not my birthstone, __[but]__ I want one anyway.

7. The diamond was square, __[and]__ it had sapphire baguettes on its sides.

8. She might give the diamond ring to her daughter, __[or]__ she might donate it to charity.

9. The diamond shimmered, __[and]__ its gold setting shone.

10. She wore no diamonds or gold, __[but]__ she looked like a princess anyway.

B. Circle the conjunction in each sentence. Underline the words the conjunction connects. Write on the line whether the conjunction connects subjects, verbs, direct objects, or sentences.

____[direct objects]____ 1. Our class art project on color required paint (and) water.

____[direct objects]____ 2. First we filled jars (and) glasses with water.

____[direct objects]____ 3. Next we gathered paints (and) brushes together.

____[subjects]____ 4. Color wheels (and) charts were hung around the room.

____[subjects]____ 5. Then the boys (and) girls had a contest.

____[direct objects]____ 6. Trudy mixed blue (and) yellow to make green.

____[direct objects]____ 7. Next Ted tried red (and) blue.

____[verbs]____ 8. He mixed (and) blended the colors to get violet.

____[direct objects]____ 9. Tara mixed red (and) green together.

____[sentences]____ 10. It didn't look like a color, (but) it did look like mud!

Prepositions, Conjunctions, Interjections

105

Name_____

100. Using Interjections

An **interjection** expresses a strong feeling or emotion. Listed below are some common interjections and the emotions they could express.

JOY	**Hurrah! Bravo! Great! Oh!**	WONDER	**Ah! Oh!**
DISGUST	**Oh! Ick! Yuck! Ugh!**	SORROW	**Oh! Ah!**
CAUTION	**Hush! Shh! Uh-oh!**	IMPATIENCE	**Goodness! Well!**
PAIN	**Oh! Ouch!**	SURPRISE	**What! Oh! Aha! Wow!**

A. Underline the interjections. Write on the line what emotion each interjection expresses. [**Possible answers are given.**]

_____[joy]_____ 1. <u>Great!</u> You're here.

_____[impatience]_____ 2. <u>Well!</u> We should be in our seats by now.

_____[wonder]_____ 3. <u>Oh!</u> This opera house is so beautiful.

_____[pain]_____ 4. <u>Ouch!</u> This seat is not so comfortable.

_____[caution]_____ 5. <u>Uh-oh!</u> The first act is about to begin.

_____[sorrow]_____ 6. <u>Oh!</u> The story is terribly sad.

_____[wonder]_____ 7. <u>Ah!</u> Her voice is very beautiful.

_____[surprise]_____ 8. <u>What!</u> It's almost over.

_____[caution]_____ 9. <u>Shh!</u> They are still singing.

_____[joy]_____ 10. They sang so well. <u>Bravo!</u>

B. Write appropriate interjections on the lines. [**Possible answers are given.**]

_____[Uh-oh!]_____ 1. Move out of the way of the bus.

_____[Ick!]_____ 2. It splashed me with that mucky water.

_____[Oh!]_____ 3. Your coat is ruined.

_____[What!]_____ 4. You have a clean one I can borrow.

_____[Hurrah!]_____ 5. Now we can still go out.

_____[Oh!]_____ 6. I don't think I can go out.

_____[Uh-oh!]_____ 7. Is something the matter?

_____[Oh!]_____ 8. I have a terrible headache.

_____[Aha!]_____ 9. I thought you weren't acting like your usual cheerful self.

_____[Ah!]_____ 10. We'll miss you if you go home.

Prepositions, Conjunctions, Interjections

Name_____

101. Reviewing Prepositions, Conjunctions, and Interjections

A. Circle the preposition in each sentence. Underline the prepositional phrase.

1. The lawyer walked (toward) the courthouse.
2. The papers (in) his case were the exhibits.
3. He had gotten home very late every night (during) the trial.
4. The judge sat (inside) his chambers.
5. They put the defendant (on) the stand.

B. Circle the correct preposition in parentheses.

1. The shirts were distributed (between (among)) the members of the team.
2. Just ((between) among) you and me, I don't like them.
3. Their color is somewhere ((between) among) green and yellow.
4. We bought them ((from) off) a dealer for a reduced price.
5. I'll take mine (from (off)) the hanger and check the price tag.

C. Write on the line whether each *italicized* phrase is adjectival or adverbial.

The tree *on the hill* was struck *by lightning*. The mishap occurred
    <u>1.</u>   <u>2.</u>

during a violent storm. It was a hot day *in August*. The dark clouds rolled
        <u>3.</u>   <u>4.</u>

across the sky. Raindrops *of enormous size* pelted the countryside. Thunder
    <u>5.</u>   <u>6.</u>

echoed *with loud booms*, and lightning darted *across the heavens*. It lasted
            <u>7.</u>   <u>8.</u>

only *for a short time*. Then the dark clouds were replaced *by a blue sky*.
        <u>9.</u>   <u>10.</u>

1. _____[adjectival]_____   6. _____[adjectival]_____

2. _____[adverbial]_____   7. _____[adverbial]_____

3. _____[adverbial]_____   8. _____[adverbial]_____

4. _____[adjectival]_____   9. _____[adverbial]_____

5. _____[adverbial]_____   10. _____[adverbial]_____

CONTINUED

D. Write on the line whether the *italicized* conjunction connects subjects, verbs, direct objects, or sentences.

___[subjects]___	1. Mike Fink *and* Paul Bunyan are folk heroes.
___[verbs]___	2. People tell *and* retell stories about them.
___[direct objects]___	3. They performed amazing feats *and* heroic deeds.
___[sentences]___	4. Mike had a great appetite, *but* Paul could eat more.
___[verbs]___	5. For breakfast Paul ate 100 pancakes *and* drank 14 gallons of milk.
___[direct objects]___	6. Paul farmed the Rocky Mountain Valley *and* the Colorado River Valley.
___[direct objects]___	7. He used Babe the Blue Ox *and* a huge plow.
___[subjects]___	8. Mike *or* Paul would have helped anyone.
___[subjects]___	9. Their strength *and* kindness were legendary.
___[sentences]___	10. Both have died, *but* their memories live on.

E. Write appropriate interjections on the lines. **[Answers will vary.]**

___[Shh!]___	1. Mike Fink is aiming for the mosquito on the fence.
___[What!]___	2. Did Mike jump across the Ohio River?
___[Wow!]___	3. Those two were amazing.
___[Hush!]___	4. She's telling the story of another folk hero.
___[Great!]___	5. I love these stories.

Try It Yourself.

Write three sentences about your favorite folktale character. Use prepositional phrases, conjunctions, and at least one interjection in your sentences.

_____

_____

_____

Check Your Own Work

Choose a selection from your writing portfolio, your journal, a work in progress, an assignment from another class, or a letter. Revise it, applying the skills you have reviewed. The checklist will help you.

✔ Have you used appropriate prepositions?

✔ Have you used *between, among, from,* and *off* correctly?

✔ Have you used interjections that express the correct emotions?

Prepositions, Conjunctions, Interjections

102. Reviewing Parts of Speech

A. Read each sentence. Identify the part of speech of each *italicized* word. Write it on the line.

noun	pronoun	verb	adjective
adverb	preposition	conjunction	interjection

____[adjective]____ 1. Atalanta was a *beautiful* maiden.

____[adverb]____ 2. She *never* wanted to marry.

____[verb]____ 3. Many men *longed* to be her husband.

____[noun]____ 4. *Atalanta* devised a plan.

____[preposition]____ 5. She was the fastest runner *in* the land.

____[pronoun]____ 6. If a man could beat *her*, he could marry her.

____[interjection]____ 7. *Ah!* Those who failed would be killed.

____[conjunction]____ 8. Suitors came from far *and* wide.

____[adverb]____ 9. Each ran well, but Atalanta *always* won.

____[pronoun]____ 10. Would *she* ever marry?

B. Complete each sentence with the part of speech indicated.
[Possible answers are given.]

adjective 1. ____[Young]____ Hippomenes decided to try.

preposition 2. He had fallen in love ____[with]____ Atalanta.

verb 3. He ____[asked]____ Venus to help him.

noun 4. Venus was the ____[Goddess]____ of Love.

adverb 5. "Help me to run ____[swiftly]____," Hippomenes begged.

pronoun 6. The Goddess had pity on ____[him]____.

noun 7. She gave him three golden ____[apples]____.

interjection 8. "____[Oh!]____ I have a chance," the youth thought.

verb 9. Hippomenes ____[walked]____ to the starting line.

conjunction 10. The signal was given, ____[and]____ the race began.

Name_____

103. Identifying Subjects and Predicates

> The **subject** names the person, place, or thing that the sentence is about.
> The **simple subject** is a noun without any of its modifiers.
>
> **The kind young <u>man</u> helped the elderly woman across the street.**
>
> The **predicate** tells what the subject is or does. The **simple predicate** is a verb without any of its modifiers, objects, or complements.
>
> **The kind young man <u>helped</u> the elderly woman across the street.**

Read each sentence. Underline the simple subject and circle the simple predicate.

1. <u>Norman Rockwell</u> (is) one of the most well-known American artists.

2. <u>He</u> (was born) in 1894 in New York City.

3. <u>He</u> (enrolled) in art school at the age of fourteen.

4. The <u>Boy Scouts of America</u> (hired) him in his late teens as the art director of its publication *Boys' Life*.

5. <u>He</u> (illustrated) more than 321 magazine covers for *The Saturday Evening Post*.

6. <u>Rockwell</u> (was interested) in civil rights and the exploration of space.

7. <u>He</u> also (was concerned) about poverty in America.

8. <u>Some</u> of his paintings (illustrate) these things.

9. <u>Most</u> of Rockwell's works (depict) everyday America.

10. <u>Rockwell's subjects</u> (include) dogs and children, baseball and barbershops.

Norman Rockwell painted and illustrated everyday America, but he also depicted things that interested or concerned him. He wanted other people to care about these things too. Give an example of how you can share one of your interests or concerns.

Name_____

104. Identifying the Complete Subject

> The subject with all its modifiers is called the **complete subject**.
>
> **The street artist with his guitar and harmonica** entertained the tourists passing by.

A. Read each sentence. Circle the simple subject and underline the complete subject.

1. The Jamestown (colonists) arrived in America in 1607.

2. The 100 male (settlers) in Jamestown had many problems.

3. The (water) near the town was bad for drinking.

4. Many dangerous (insects) lived around the swampy colony.

5. Insect (bites) caused disease among the settlers.

6. The (men) in the colony didn't know how to hunt or fish.

7. The (people) of Jamestown asked John Smith to be their leader.

8. The resourceful (Smith) helped the people work together to survive.

9. The grateful (colonists) began to store food for the winter.

10. Some helpful American (Indians) taught the colonists to grow corn.

B. Complete each sentence with a descriptive adjective or an adjectival phrase. Put parentheses around the complete subjects. **[Possible answers are given.]**

1. (The ice _____[on the pond]_____) has thawed.

2. (The ice skates _____[in the closet]_____) can't be used.

3. (The _____[deep]_____ snow) has almost disappeared.

4. (The trees _____[in the neighborhood]_____) will soon have tiny buds.

5. (The birds _____[down south]_____) will soon fly north.

Sentences

111

105. Identifying the Complete Predicate

> The predicate with all its modifiers, objects, and complements is called the **complete predicate**.
>
> **The hungry child ate pizza, pasta, and salad for dinner.**

A. Read each sentence. Circle the simple predicate and underline the complete predicate.

1. Most of the settlers in the New England colonies (arrived) there from England.

2. They (lived) in villages like their old ones in England.

3. Many villages (had) a meeting house in the center.

4. The settlers (used) the meeting house as a church.

5. They (talked) about village problems there.

6. The Middle Colonies (had) good land for farming.

7. The people in these colonies (came) from many different lands.

8. They (practiced) many different religions.

9. Colonists in New York (spoke) eighteen different languages.

10. Colonists in the Middle Colonies (sold) wheat to people in other colonies.

B. Complete the sentences with modifiers, objects, or complements. Put parentheses around the complete predicates. **[Possible answers given.]**

1. Gerald (was given _____ [the athletic award.])

2. Ken (ate _____ [pancakes and sausage for breakfast.])

3. Catherine (wrote _____ [the essay.])

4. Lightning (streaked _____ [across the sky.])

5. The tourists (crowded _____ [into the bus.])

6. Mike (told _____ [me the secret.])

7. Weeds (grew _____ [in the flower garden.])

8. The car (stopped _____ [at the corner.])

9. The terrier (bounded _____ [across the field.])

10. The pilot (climbed _____ [into the plane.])

Sentences

106. Recognizing Complete Sentences

A **sentence** is a group of words that expresses a complete thought.
Every sentence has a subject and a predicate.

SUBJECT   PREDICATE

That busy lawyer   devotes some of her time to charity work.

A. Read each example. Write **S** on the line if the words form a sentence.
Write **NS** on the line if the words do not form a sentence.

___[NS]___ 1. Many years ago.

___[S]___ 2. The pioneers traveled in covered wagons.

___[NS]___ 3. Sometimes large families and even a dog.

___[NS]___ 4. Early in the morning.

___[S]___ 5. They made bread in cast iron pans.

___[NS]___ 6. Often slept under their wagons.

___[S]___ 7. Some of the wagons were pulled by oxen.

___[NS]___ 8. Met Indians on the plains.

___[NS]___ 9. Became sick on their journey.

___[NS]___ 10. No doctor to help them.

___[NS]___ 11. The dangerous snow-covered mountains.

___[S]___ 12. The deserts were very hard on the animals.

___[S]___ 13. Occasionally the pioneers became lost.

___[S]___ 14. Many of the pioneers were immigrants.

___[NS]___ 15. Founded new towns out west.

B. Write a complete sentence using each group of words.
Be sure to start each sentence with a capital letter and
end it with the correct punctuation mark. **[Sentences will vary.]**

when it rains   1. _____

alone at night   2. _____

in the attic   3. _____

is scary   4. _____

in the mirror   5. _____

Sentences

Name_____

107. Forming Compound Subjects

> If a sentence has two or more simple subjects, it is said
> to have a **compound subject**.
>
> **The <u>student</u> and <u>teacher</u> discussed the assignment after class.**

A. Read each sentence. Underline the compound subject.
Circle the conjunction.

1. Grapes (and) peaches grow on that farm.

2. Fruits (and) vegetables are a good source of vitamins.

3. Not Brendan (but) Juan fed apples to the horses.

4. California (and) Florida have many orange groves.

5. Strawberries (and) rhubarb were in that delicious pie.

6. Carrots (and) sweet potatoes are orange in color.

7. Rabbits (and) guinea pigs eat lettuce.

8. Insects (or) droughts can ruin vegetable crops.

9. Corn (and) pumpkins are sold at the roadside market.

10. Nicole (and) her family picked blueberries in Michigan.

11. Everyone (but) Tony brought a piece of fruit for lunch.

12. The cows (and) horses are kept in separate barns.

13. Ducks (and) geese swim in the pond near the farm.

14. Broccoli (or) carrots are good additions on a salad

15. Corn (and) soybeans are the chief crops of Nebraska and Illinois.

B. Complete each sentence with a compound subject. [Possible answers are given.]

1. _____[Nick]_____ and _____[Alex]_____ have gone to the airport.

2. _____[Grandma]_____ and _____[Grandpa]_____ are coming to visit.

3. The _____[suitcases]_____ and the _____[wheelchair]_____ just fit in the trunk.

4. _____[They]_____ and _____[our parents]_____ will have lots to talk about.

5. _____[Dad]_____ and _____[I]_____ will take Grandpa for a walk.

Sentences

108. Forming Compound Predicates

> If a sentence has two or more verbs, it is said to have
> a **compound predicate**.
> **A clever and malicious thief <u>stole</u> and <u>destroyed</u> the famous painting.**

A. Underline the compound simple predicate in each sentence.
Circle the conjunction.

1. The patients <u>sat</u> (and) <u>waited</u> for the doctor.

2. Their friends and spouses <u>cheered</u> (and) <u>comforted</u> them.

3. The busy orderlies <u>came</u> (and) <u>went</u> through
   the emergency room doors.

4. Those doors <u>opened</u> (and) <u>closed</u> frequently.

5. The victim <u>was undressed</u> (and) then
   <u>was examined</u> by the doctors.

6. He <u>yelled</u> (and) <u>cried</u> in pain when they touched him.

7. The pregnant woman <u>sweated</u> (and) <u>breathed</u> hard during delivery.

8. The premature baby <u>did not kick</u> (or) <u>scream</u> as other babies do.

9. The mother <u>nurses</u> (or) <u>feeds</u> the baby with a bottle.

10. The father <u>talks</u> (and) <u>sings</u> to the baby.

B. Read the sentences. Combine each pair of sentences
into one sentence with a compound predicate. **[Possible answers are given.]**

1. The teacher stacked the tests on her desk. She wrote the directions on the board.

   [The teacher stacked the tests on her desk and wrote the directions on the board.]

2. The student cleared his desk. The student sharpened his pencil.

   [The student cleared his desk and sharpened his pencil.]

3. After the test put your pencils down. After the test turn your papers over.

   [After the test put your pencils down and turn your papers over.]

4. Now we'll review our tests. Now we'll correct our mistakes.

   [Now we'll review our tests and correct our mistakes.]

5. The student reached for his test. The student smiled when he saw it.

   [The student reached for his test and smiled when he saw it.]

Name_____

109. Forming Compound Objects

> If a verb has two or more direct objects, it is said to have
> a **compound direct object**.
>
> **In gym class we played basketball and floor hockey.**

A. Underline the compound direct object in each sentence.
Circle the conjunction.

1. We will visit the Sears Tower (or) the John Hancock Building
   in Chicago.

2. Visitors to New York can see the Statue of Liberty
   (but) not the Eiffel Tower.

3. In London buy a postcard (or) a model of Big Ben,
   one of London's famous landmarks.

4. Venice's St. Mark's Square boasts many tourists (and) pigeons.

5. Can you envision Rome's Coliseum (and) Athens's Parthenon?

6. Photograph the Sphinx (and) the Great Pyramid when you tour Egypt.

7. Research Falling Water (or) Taliesin to find out about
   Frank Lloyd Wright's architecture.

8. Read the rules (and) regulations carefully before entering
   the Taj Mahal, a beautiful building in Agra, India.

9. The Eiffel Tower in Paris attracts many tourists (but) few locals.

10. See every nook (and) cranny of Sagrada Familia (Holy Family),
    that famous church in Barcelona.

B. Complete each sentence with a compound object. **[Possible answers are given.]**

1. Do you have a _____[pencil]_____ or a _____[pen]_____?

2. I am writing a short _____[story]_____ or a _____[poem]_____.

3. A writer needs _____[paper]_____ to write on or a _____[computer]_____
   to type on.

4. That topic makes _____[adults]_____ and _____[children]_____ alike
   think seriously.

5. Ask a _____[magazine]_____ or _____[newspaper]_____ to publish your work.

Sentences

116

Name_____

110. Reviewing Compound Elements in a Sentence

A. Underline the compound element in each sentence. Write on the line whether the subject, predicate, or direct object is compound.

__[subject]__ 1. Columbus and his crew left Spain on August 3, 1492.

__[subject]__ 2. The *Niña*, the *Pinta*, and the *Santa Maria* sailed west.

__[predicate]__ 3. The crew raised and lowered the sails.

__[predicate]__ 4. They cleaned the deck and fixed things on the ship.

__[predicate]__ 5. After a month at sea the crew worried and complained.

__[subject]__ 6. Columbus and the sailors were afraid.

__[predicate]__ 7. Columbus steered the ship and wrote in his log.

__[subject]__ 8. Winds and waves made the voyage dangerous.

__[direct object]__ 9. Finally the crew saw land and trees in the distance.

__[predicate]__ 10. They landed and named the new land San Salvador.

__[direct object]__ 11. The people on San Salvador grew yams and corn.

__[direct object]__ 12. They greeted Columbus and his men.

__[direct object]__ 13. They brought food and water to the sailors.

__[direct object]__ 14. The sailors gave beads and bells to the Indians.

__[subject]__ 15. The sailors and the Indians learned from each other.

B. Write a sentence using each compound element. [Sentences will vary.]

jump and play 1. _____

Mae and Jeff 2. _____

cake and pie 3. _____

rain and hail 4. _____

drew and painted 5. _____

Sentences

117

111. Recognizing Natural and Inverted Order in Sentences

A sentence is in **natural order** when the verb follows the subject.

The little house stood on the prairie.

A sentence is in **inverted order** when the verb or an auxiliary verb comes before the subject.

On the prairie stood the little house.

Underline the simple subject and circle the simple predicate.
Write **N** if the sentence is in natural order and **I** if the sentence is in inverted order.

___[I]___ 1. Many centuries ago (lived) the Anasazi.

___[N]___ 2. Anasazi (is) a Navajo Indian word meaning "ancient ones."

___[N]___ 3. Some of their ruins (are) in Colorado's Mesa Verde National Park.

___[N]___ 4. In the high cliffs of the Mesa Verde area they (built) cliff dwellings.

___[I]___ 5. Four stories high (stood) some of these dwellings.

___[N]___ 6. They (used) ladders to enter their cliff homes.

___[I]___ 7. In the winter, bitterly cold (were) these homes.

___[N]___ 8. The Anasazi (were called) Basket Makers.

___[N]___ 9. They (excelled) at basketry.

___[I]___ 10. Waterproof (were) some of their baskets.

___[N]___ 11. The archaeologists (dug) under the kiva, a cliff dwelling's underground room.

___[I]___ 12. Through the kiva (whipped) the wind.

___[I]___ 13. Below the cliff dwellings (lies) a trash area.

___[N]___ 14. Pinyon pines and Juniper trees (grew) in the area.

___[N]___ 15. The Anasazi farms (lay) on top of the mesa.

112. Reviewing the Four Kinds of Sentences

There are four kinds of sentences—
declarative, interrogative, imperative, and exclamatory.

A **declarative sentence** makes a statement. It ends with a period.

> **The weather is beautiful today.**

An **interrogative sentence** asks a question. It ends with a question mark.

> **Will I need my umbrella?**

An **imperative sentence** gives a command or makes a request.
It ends with a period.

> **Wear this waterproof jacket.**

An **exclamatory sentence** expresses strong emotion.
It ends with an exclamation point.

> **I told you not to go out in the rain!**

Add the end punctuation to each sentence. Decide whether
the sentence is declarative, interrogative, imperative, or exclamatory.
Write your answer on the line.

[interrogative] 1. Have you ever read Greek mythology [?]

[imperative] 2. Name some of the ancient gods and goddesses [.]

[exclamatory] 3. How fascinating the stories are [!]

[declarative] 4. My favorite myth is about Medusa [.]

[interrogative] 5. Do you know the god of war [?]

[declarative] 6. Pegasus is a horse with wings [.]

[imperative] 7. Name a mythological creature [.]

[exclamatory] 8. How mighty Zeus was [!]

[interrogative] 9. Is Venus the goddess of love [?]

[exclamatory] 10. What a fearsome creature is the Minotaur [!]

[interrogative] 11. Who was the boy who tried to fly [?]

[declarative] 12. Hercules was a Greek hero known for his great strength [.]

[imperative] 13. List Hercules' twelve labors [.]

[exclamatory] 14. How angry Hera gets [!]

[interrogative] 15. Did Argus, the hundred-eyed monster, see you [?]

Sentences

119

Name_____

113. Writing Different Kinds of Sentences

Rewrite each sentence in the form indicated. **[Possible answers are given.]**

1. Is Tom's closet cluttered?

   exclamatory: _____ [How cluttered Tom's closet is!] _____

2. The clutter includes things from when he was very young.

   interrogative: _____ [Does the clutter include things from when he was very young?] _____

3. Is that where his baseball mitt was?

   exclamatory: _____ [That is where his baseball mitt was!] _____

4. Doesn't he wish he hadn't thrown all that stuff in there?

   declarative: _____ [He wishes he hadn't thrown all that stuff in there.] _____

5. Does he use an air freshener in there?

   imperative: _____ [Use an air freshener in there.] _____

6. Here's his favorite baseball card.

   exclamatory: _____ [Here's his favorite baseball card!] _____

7. Does he want some help going through things?

   declarative: _____ [He wants some help going through things.] _____

8. We should throw this old bag in the garbage.

   interrogative: _____ [Should we throw this old bag in the garbage?] _____

9. This sweatshirt looks brand new.

   interrogative: _____ [Does this sweatshirt look brand new?] _____

10. Are you touching that mousetrap?

    imperative: _____ [Don't touch that mousetrap.] _____

_____

Sentences

Name_____

114. Reviewing Sentences

A. Read each sentence. Write **CS** if the *italicized* words are
a complete subject or **CP** if they are a complete predicate.
Write your answers on the lines.

___[CS]___ 1. *A ferocious mile-wide tornado* descended upon the town.

___[CP]___ 2. Debris *swirled around its funnel cloud.*

___[CP]___ 3. Its loud roar *echoed in the night.*

___[CP]___ 4. Trees and bushes *were leveled by the force of its winds.*

___[CS]___ 5. *Its massive force* tore homes into pieces.

B. Read each sentence. Write **S** on the line if
the words form a sentence. Write **NS** on the line
if the words do not form a sentence.

___[NS]___ 1. Skipping through the woods
on a spring morning.

___[S]___ 2. The wolf peered from behind a tree.

___[S]___ 3. Each flower caught Red Riding
Hood's attention.

___[NS]___ 4. A large bouquet for Grandmother.

___[S]___ 5. To Grandmother's house she went.

C. Decide whether each sentence is declarative,
interrogative, imperative, or exclamatory. Write your
answers on the lines. Then underline the simple subject
and circle the simple predicate.

_____[declarative]_____ 1. <u>Atalanta</u> (ran) far ahead of Hippomenes.

_____[interrogative]_____ 2. (Could) <u>Hippomenes</u> possibly (win)?

_____[imperative]_____ 3. (Help) me now, Venus.

_____[declarative]_____ 4. The <u>youth</u> (threw) a golden apple far ahead.

_____[exclamatory]_____ 5. Ah, <u>it</u> (caught) Atalanta's attention!

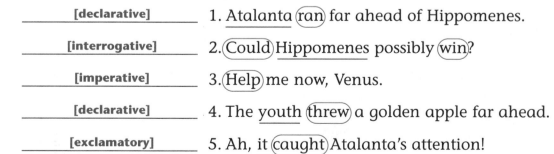

_____[interrogative]_____ 6. (Would) she (pick) up the apple?

_____[exclamatory]_____ 7. Yes, Atalanta (did!)

_____[imperative]_____ 8. (Take) advantage of this, Hippomenes.

_____[declarative]_____ 9. Hippomenes and Atalanta (were) side by side.

_____[declarative]_____ 10. Hippomenes (aimed) and (threw) the remaining apples.

D. Read each sentence. Write **CS** if the *italicized* words form a compound subject, **CP** if they form a compound predicate, or **CO** if they form a compound object. Write your answers on the lines.

Write **N** over the sentence if it is in natural order or **I** if it is in inverted order.

___[CS]___ 1. Inside Atalanta fought good
                 [I]
         judgment and *foolishness*.

___[CP]___ 2. She *wavered* and *picked* them up.
                [N]

___[CO]___ 3. Hippomenes saw *hope* and *victory*
                 [N]
         within his grasp.

___[CP]___ 4. He *reached* and *crossed* the finish line first.
                [N]

___[CO]___ 5. He had won for himself a *race* and a *bride*!
                [N]

Try It Yourself

Write four sentences about a game or contest you have seen.
Be sure to use complete sentences and correct punctuation.

_____

_____

_____

_____

Check Your Own Work

Choose a selection from your writing portfolio, your journal,
a work in progress, an assignment from another class, or a letter.
Revise it, applying the skills you have reviewed. The checklist
will help you.

✔ Do all your sentences express a complete thought?

✔ Have you used a variety of sentences—declarative, interrogative,
imperative, and exclamatory?

115. Using Periods

Use a **period** at the end of a declarative or an imperative sentence, after most abbreviations, and after an initial.

Raul walked to school today in the rain.
Pick that up off the ground.
Reverend   Rev.
Alex Mark Moore   A. M. Moore

Abbreviations for units of measure and the two-letter state postal abbreviations do not use periods. Only the abbreviation for *inch* uses a period.

centimeter   cm   Colorado   CO

A. Write the correct abbreviation for each word. Use periods where needed.

1. kilometer ___[km]___   6. before noon ___[A.M.]___

2. ounce ___[oz]___   7. President ___[Pres.]___

3. please reply ___[R. S. V. P.]___   8. Tuesday ___[Tues.]___

4. General ___[Gen.]___   9. California ___[CA]___

5. New Jersey ___[NJ]___   10. feet ___[ft]___

B. Add periods where needed.

1. Charles J.H. Dickens is a well-known English author .

2. He was born in Portsmouth on Feb.7, 1812 .

3. His writing, editing, touring, etc. kept him busy .

4. In A.D.1836 Dickens married Catherine Hogarth .

5. He had remarkable energy; sometimes he walked thirty miles into Kent .

6. In his books he immortalized his father as Mr.Micawber .

7. Mrs.Nickleby was based on his mother .

8. In Jan.1842, Dickens visited the U.S.mainland .

9. Dr.Oliver W.Holmes organized a welcome for him in Boston .

10. H.W.Longfellow and W.E.Channing attended the affair .

C. Rewrite each person's name, using initials for the *italicized* words.

1. Robert *Louis* Stevenson   [Robert L. Stevenson]

2. *George Bernard* Shaw   [G. B. Shaw]

3. *Louisa May Alcott*   [L. M. A.]

4. *Ralph* Waldo Emerson   [R. Waldo Emerson]

5. Edgar *Allan* Poe   [Edgar A. Poe]

Name_____

116. Using Commas in a Series and in Parts of a Letter

> **Commas** are used to separate words in a series.
>
> **At the store pick up some butter, bread, and bananas.**
> **Kurt, Ray, and Mike are going to the game together.**
>
> Commas also follow the salutation and complimentary close of a letter.
>
> **Dear Coach Peters,**
> **Sincerely,**

A. Add commas where needed.

1. Breakfast,lunch,and dinner should never be skipped.

2. Mom used her Irish linen tablecloth,her German china,and her English silver.

3. Tom put cereal,juice,yogurt,and bagels on the table.

4. Mom served cherry streusel,banana cream pie,and cheese coffee cakes.

5. Quinn can make scrambled,poached,and hardboiled eggs.

6. In the picnic basket were sandwiches,fruit,pretzels,and lemonade.

7. Dad bought carrots,lettuce,radishes,and cucumbers for the dinner salad.

8. The recipe said to shake,beat,stir,and then boil the various ingredients.

9. Corn,peas,and potatoes are my favorite vegetables.

10. Martha stretched,pulled,kneaded,and rolled out the dough.

11. Dear Mom and Dad ,

12. Your friend ,

13. My dear Aunt Bridget ,

14. Love ,

15. Your son ,

B. Complete each sentence with a series of nouns, verbs, or adjectives. Add commas where needed.

1. ____[noun,]____ ____[noun,]____ and ____[noun]____ are my favorite rides at the amusement park.   **[Answers will vary.]**

2. I can see ____[noun,]____ ____[noun,]____ and ____[noun]____ at the fairgrounds.

3. Do you ____[verb,]____ ____[verb,]____ and ____[verb]____ at the beach?

4. The colors of the balloons were ____[adjective,]____ ____[adjective,]____ and ____[adjective]____ .

5. I eat ____[noun,]____ ____[noun,]____ and ____[noun]____ at the festival.

Name_____

117. Using Commas with Dates and Geographical Names

Place a comma between the day of the month and the year.
Do not use a comma when only the month and year are given.

The weather was harsh on January 22, 2001.
The heaviest rains fell in April 1998.

Place a comma after the year unless it comes at the end of the sentence.

The date October 12, 1492, is important in American history.
Columbus landed in America on October 12, 1492.

Place a comma between the name of a city and a state or country. Place a comma after the name of the state or a country unless it comes at the end of the sentence.

Rome, Italy, is the home of the famous Coliseum.
The famous Coliseum's home is Rome, Italy.

Add commas where needed.

1. U. S. Grant was born on April 22, 1822.

2. On December 16, 1773, the Boston Tea Party occurred.

3. At Plymouth, Massachusetts, the Pilgrims celebrated the first Thanksgiving.

4. Detroit, Michigan, is the center of the automobile industry.

5. The United States Navy was established on October 13, 1775.

6. France gave the United States the Statue of Liberty on October 28, 1886.

7. The Declaration of Independence was signed in Independence Hall, Philadelphia, Pennsylvania.

8. My best friend lives in Portland, Oregon.

9. There is a house shaped like an elephant in Margate, New Jersey.

10. Many pyramids still stand in El Giza, Egypt.

11. Have you ever visited Warsaw, Poland?

12. On May 29, 1953, Sir Edmund Hillary reached the summit of Mt. Everest.

13. On July 20, 1969, Neil Armstrong collected rock samples on the moon.

14. Christopher Columbus sailed from Spain on August 3, 1492.

15. The first permanent English settlement was established in Jamestown, Virginia, in 1607.

Punctuation & Capitalization

125

Name_____

118. Using Commas with <u>Yes</u> and <u>No</u> and with Words in Direct Address

Commas are used after the words *yes* and *no* when they introduce sentences.

Yes, you may go bike riding.   No, it's too late to go out.

Commas are also used to separate words in direct address. When the name of a person addressed is the first word of a sentence, it is followed by a comma. If it is the last word of a sentence, a comma is placed before the name.

Tony, let's go.   Where would you like me to put this, Chris?

If the name of the person is used within a sentence, one comma is placed before the name and one after the name.

I hope you know, Gina, how much I appreciate your help.

A. Read each sentence. Add commas where needed.

1. Yes, seals and penguins can be found in Antarctic waters.

2. Seals, Jackie, have a layer of fat that keeps them warm in cold water.

3. Did you read the chapter on animals of the Antarctic, Kevin?

4. Boys and girls, can you name some kinds of seals?

5. No, not all seals have external ears.

6. Trina, the female seal is called a cow.

7. Can you tell me what the male seal is called, class?

8. Yes, the male seal is called a bull.

9. Usually, Eric, the cow has just one pup per breeding season.

10. Yes, the leopard seal sometimes feeds on penguins.

11. Penguins live in groups called rookeries, Paige.

12. The male penguins, David, hold the eggs on their feet.

13. No, the females do not guard the eggs.

14. Yes, penguins are heavy birds.

15. This makes them good divers and swimmers, Colette.

B. Complete each sentence with a noun in direct address. Use correct punctuation. **[Answers will vary.]**

1. Ernest Shackleton ____[, Name,]____ explored the South Pole.

2. His ship was called the *Endurance* ____[, Name]____ .

3. The *Endurance* ____[, Name,]____ got trapped in the ice.

4. Eventually ____[, Name,]____ the ship was crushed by the ice and sank.

5. ____[Name,]____ can you imagine being stranded in a lifeboat in those icy waters?

119. Using Commas with Quotation Marks

Commas and **quotation marks** are used to set off short direct quotations.

Place a comma after the exact words of the speaker when they come at the beginning of the sentence.

> **"Ron, please help me plant this tree," begged Ben.**

Place a comma before the exact words of the speaker when they come at the end of the sentence.

> **The teacher said very clearly, "Put your pencils down."**

If the exact words of the speaker are divided, two commas are used to separate the quotation from the rest of the sentence.

> **"Our team," exclaimed Sherry, "won by thirty points!"**

A. Add commas where needed.

1. The children shouted, "Let's make a snowman!"
2. Lilly suggested, "How about a snow family?"
3. Alex said, "That's a great idea!"
4. "Chris, help me gather twigs for their arms," called Sam.
5. "Look," shouted Nicholas, "at the size of its body!"
6. Lilly said, "Let's make this one the father snowman."
7. "Can you help me," asked Alex, "roll this closer?"
8. "Does anyone," questioned Chris, "have old hats?"
9. Lilly interrupted, "Let's go to my house to look for some hats."
10. "Maybe we can have some hot chocolate," responded Nicholas.
11. "The hot chocolate is great, Mrs. Tan!" exclaimed Sam.
12. "I'll bake cookies," promised Mrs. Tan, "by the time you're done."
13. "I found some hats and a bonnet," called Lilly.
14. "Here are some carrots for the noses," offered Mrs. Tan.
15. "Thanks, Mrs. Tan!" replied the children.

B. Complete each sentence with a speaker and verb. Add commas where needed.

1. _____[Answers will vary.]_____ "What a snow storm we are having!"
2. "The sled," _____ "is in the closet."
3. "Don't forget your hat and gloves," _____.
4. "It's fun," _____ "to make snowmen."
5. _____ "I heard that it will stop snowing by morning."

120. Using Commas with Conjunctions

> Commas are used before the conjunctions *and*, *but*, and *or* when two simple sentences are combined.
>
> **Some of the children went to art class, but others went to the gym.**

A. Read each sentence. Add commas where needed.

1. Marie likes to use paint for her art, and Erica likes to use pastels.
2. She redrew the figure, but it still wasn't right.
3. We will finish our paintings in class, or we will finish them at home.
4. The critic didn't like her drawings, but he liked her sculptures.
5. They put their paints away, and then they cleaned their brushes.

B. Read each sentence. Use a conjunction to complete each sentence. Add commas where needed.

1. Fold your paper into four equal parts __[, and]__ then you can draw a favorite book character in each section.
2. I will draw Huck Finn in one of the sections __[, and/, but]__ I don't know who will go in the other sections.
3. Huck had a friend named Jim __[, or]__ was his name John?
4. Read *Huckleberry Finn* __[, or]__ you will miss a good story.
5. Mark Twain wrote *Huckleberry Finn* __[, but/, and]__ that is not all he wrote.

C. Combine each set of simple sentences with a conjunction. Add commas where needed.

1. There was a long wait to ride the roller-coaster. You could get on the bumper cars immediately.

   [There was a long wait to ride the roller coaster, but you could get on the bumper cars immediately.]

2. Don't eat too much candy. You might feel ill on the rides.

   [Don't eat too much candy, or you might feel ill on the rides.]

3. We ate lunch. Then we went on the train ride.

   [We ate lunch, and then we went on the train ride.]

4. Henry's favorite ride is the Wild Eagle. Julia enjoys the Twirly Whirly.

   [Henry's favorite ride is the Wild Eagle, and Julia enjoys the Twirly Whirly.]

5. The Wild Eagle is fun. The Twirly Whirly can be scary.

   [The Wild Eagle is fun, but the Twirly Whirly can be scary.]

Name_____

121. Reviewing Commas

Read each sentence. Add commas where needed.

1. Class, you were to write a report on Florence Nightingale, Madam C. J. Walker, or Clara Barton.

2. "I picked Madam C. J. Walker because she was one of our first American businesswomen," Tory said.

3. "Did you know," asked Tory, "that she was born in Louisiana in 1867?"

4. "In 1887 she moved to St. Louis, Missouri, Rob."

5. "There, class, she learned about the world from other African-American women who belonged to the National Association of Colored Women."

6. "Around 1904," Tory explained, "she developed a scalp condition and lost her hair."

7. "She tried a particular treatment, and she went to work for that company in Denver, Colorado, Rob."

8. "She married Charles Joseph Walker," Mrs. Hobson said, "and they became business partners."

9. "They sold a scalp conditioner called Madam C. J. Walker's Wonderful Hair Grower, Lisa."

10. "Did you know, Steven, that Madam C. J. Walker promoted her products by going door-to-door with them in the South?" asked Erin.

11. "She became a successful businesswoman, class."

12. "I read that she shared her success by donating $1,000 to the building fund of the black people's YMCA in Indianapolis," offered Rob.

13. Leon said, "She also gave $5,000 to the NAACP's antilynching movement."

14. Erin added, "She also encouraged those who worked for her to care about their country and to be politically active."

15. Madam C. J. Walker said, "If I have accomplished anything in life, it is because I have been willing to work hard."

Madam C. J. Walker worked hard to become a successful businesswoman. Give an example of how you can work hard to be successful at something.

Name_____

122. Using Exclamation Points, Question Marks, and Apostrophes

An **exclamation point** is used at the end of a sentence that expresses a strong feeling; it is also used after a word or phrase that expresses a strong feeling.

There's a car coming; get out of the way!   **Ouch!**

A **question mark** is used at the end of every interrogative sentence.

What could have happened to Margie?

An **apostrophe** is used to show ownership or possession. It is also used in a contraction to mark the place where a letter or letters have been omitted.

**the young man's guitar   those girls' guitars
don't (do not)   can't (cannot)**

A. Add exclamation points and questions marks where needed.

1. Hurry up! Mom and Dad are waiting in the car !
2. Did you remember to bring your camera ?
3. What an exciting day this is !
4. Are we really going to the Everglades ?
5. Did you know that Everglades National Park is the only place in the world where alligators and crocodiles live together in the same habitat ?

B. Add apostrophes where needed to show possession.

1. We could see a crocodile's eyes just above the water.
2. Mangrove trees' decomposed leaves are elements in the food web of the Everglades.
3. Many alligators' nests lie among the roots of the mangrove.
4. A mangrove's roots offer homes for other birds and fish.
5. Humans' attempts to manage the water in south Florida have endangered the Everglades.

C. Write the contraction for each pair of words.

1. does not ___[doesn't]___
2. are not ___[aren't]___
3. did not ___[didn't]___
4. will not ___[won't]___
5. we have ___[we've]___
6. I will ___[I'll]___
7. we will ___[we'll]___
8. you have ___[you've]___
9. would not ___[wouldn't]___
10. could not ___[couldn't]___

Punctuation & Capitalization

130

123. Using Punctuation in Direct Quotations

Quotation marks are used before and after a direct quotation.

> "We have more of these in stock," offered the salesperson.

A comma is placed before or after a direct quotation.

> The policeman warned, "Wear your seatbelt at all times."
> "The story had interesting characters," remarked Lucy.

If the quotation ends with a question mark or exclamation point, the comma is not used.

> "Must you wear that dirty sweatshirt?" Mother asked.
> "I won the prize!" cried Michael.

A. Add quotation marks and other punctuation where needed.

1. "Who wants to go to the botanical gardens?" inquired William.

2. "I would like to see the spring flowers there," replied his sister Lindsay.

3. "Let's get in the car," Mom said.

4. "Buckle your seat belts," instructed Mom.

5. "This plant is very fragile," cautioned the botanist.

6. Lindsay remarked, "It's beautiful!"

7. "Where does it grow?" asked William.

8. The botanist answered, "It grows primarily on the Pacific islands."

9. William questioned, "Like Hawaii?"

10. "Yes, it is very common there," said the botanist.

11. The botanist continued, "These plants should bloom in another week."

12. "Do you have bushes that are shaped like animals?" questioned Lindsay.

13. Mom stated, "I just saw a sign that said they are down the path."

14. The botanist suggested, "You can take a shortcut through this greenhouse."

15. "Thanks for all the information!" they shouted.

B. Complete each sentence with the exact words of the speaker.
Add quotation marks and punctuation where needed. **[Answers will vary.]**

1. _____ shouted the first baseman.

2. Miguel cried _____

3. Emily asked _____

4. _____ pleaded the class.

5. _____ said the teacher.

124. Using Punctuation in Divided Quotations

> Quotation marks are used before and after every part of a divided quotation.
>
> **"King Montezuma," said the guide, "drank fifty cups of chocolate a day."**

A. Add quotation marks and punctuation where needed.

1. "This is not," Paul muttered, "my favorite pastime."
2. "Oh, really," asked Gillian, "what would you rather be doing?"
3. "I'd much rather," responded Paul, "be outside on my bike."
4. "Gillian," asked Paul, "wouldn't you rather be doing something else too?"
5. "Sure I would," said Gillian, "but we promised Mom we'd help her get ready for the party."
6. "Right," agreed Paul, "we sure did."
7. "Do you think," asked Paul, "that we've cut up enough vegetables?"
8. "Yes, I think," said Gillian, "that we've prepared enough for the tray."
9. "Now what we need to do," stated Paul, "is make the dip."
10. "No," returned Gillian, "I've already made it."
11. "Okay," Paul asked, "what else can we do for Mom?"
12. "I'd say," offered Gillian, "that we could sweep the floors."
13. "And it wouldn't hurt," he continued, "to vacuum the rugs."
14. "I'd be happy to do the vacuuming," said Paul, "if you do the sweeping."
15. "Mom will be so pleased," stated Gillian, "when she sees how much we've done."

B. Complete each sentence with the exact words of the speaker. Add quotation marks and punctuation where needed. **[Answers will vary.]**

1. _____ Joseph explained _____
2. _____ announced Anna _____
3. _____ said Darnell _____
4. _____ encouraged the coach _____
5. _____ the butcher replied _____

125. Quotation Marks and Underlining in Titles

Quotation marks are used to enclose the titles of stories, poems, and TV shows.

STORY	"The Scarlet Ibis"
POEM	"The Other Side of the Door"
TV SHOW	"Crocodile Hunter"

Titles of books, movies, and works of art are printed in italics.
When you write the title of a book or work of art, underline the title
since you cannot write in italics.

BOOK	*The Secret Garden*	<u>The Secret Garden</u>
MOVIE	*Star Wars*	<u>Star Wars</u>
PAINTING	*Mona Lisa*	<u>Mona Lisa</u>

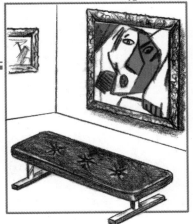

A. Add quotation marks and underlining where needed.

1. Have you read the poem "Tug of War" by Kathleen Fraser?
2. Let's watch "Teen Talent Show" on television tonight.
3. <u>The Seeing Summer</u> is a beautiful book about a blind girl.
4. Which artist painted <u>Whistling Boy</u>?
5. "Valentine for Earth" is a delightful poem by Francis Frost.
6. I enjoyed reading the short story "Bowleg Bill, Cowboy of the Ocean Waves."
7. Does the library have the book <u>Old Yeller</u>?
8. Draw a picture after you have read the poem "Subways Are People."
9. The girl in the painting <u>Girl with Watering Can</u> looks like my little sister.
10. If I do my homework before dinner, I can watch "Lovable Laughs."
11. If you want to read a funny book, try <u>Homer Price</u> by Robert McCloskey.
12. Read Ray Bradbury's short story "The Wonderful Ice Cream Suit."
13. The painting <u>Snap the Whip</u> looks like the real thing.
14. You won't be able to put down the book <u>They Lived with the Dinosaurs.</u>
15. If you like the ocean, you'll enjoy the poem "Shells" by Lilian Moore.

B. Complete each sentence with appropriate information.
Add quotation marks and underlining where needed. **[Answers will vary.]**

1. _____ is my favorite book.
2. Do you like the poem _____?
3. My favorite TV show is _____.
4. Our class went to the museum and saw the painting _____.
5. In our reader we just finished the story _____.

Name_____

126. Using Capital Letters

Capital letters are used for
- the first word in a sentence
- proper nouns and proper adjectives
- abbreviations when capital letters would be used if the words were written in full
- initials
- important words in titles of books, plays, poems, art objects, and compositions
- the first word in a direct quotation
- the first word of a line of poetry
- names of deities, the Bible, and other sacred books
- North, South, East, and West when they refer to sections of a country
- the first word in a salutation and the name of the person addressed
- the first word in the complimentary close of a letter
- the pronoun *I* and the interjection *O*

A. Use the proofreading symbol (≡) to show which letters should be capitalized.

1. my family and i went to my aunt's house in illinois for thanksgiving.
2. in vermont the hunting season began last tuesday.
3. mr. a. j. miller attended a convention in perry, ohio.
4. i wrote a poem called "the winds of kansas."
5. "corn," said the farmer, "is the chief crop in this part of indiana."
6. have you read the book *appalachia: the voices of sleeping birds*?
7. the native americans named manhattan island.
8. my mom has an authentic hawaiian grass skirt.
9. you drive through nebraska to get to colorado from iowa.
10. "here we are!" exclaimed madeline. "we finally made it to maine."
11. is there a poem about alabama in the book *poems about your home*?
12. charles a. lindbergh flew from new york to paris.
13. i can remember being fascinated by mexican jumping beans.
14. my dear uncle fred,
15. last summer, tom and i took a trip to kalamazoo, michigan.

B. Circle the groups of words that are capitalized correctly.

1. The Landing Of The Pilgrims
2. Dear aunt Veronica,
3. (I live in the South.)
4. (Battersby Street)
5. "Macavity The Mystery Cat"
6. (the American flag)
7. (Westtown School)
8. Your Friend,
9. Mrs. Fern a. Loftus
10. (Declaration of Independence)

Punctuation & Capitalization

134

Name_____

127. Reviewing Punctuation and Capitalization

A. Add periods where needed.

1. M.C.Johnson began a new business .

2. Nov.is the abbreviation for November .

3. What famous battle occurred in A.D.1066?

4. Dr.Horn arrived at the hospital at 3:55 A.M .

5. Workers at the Pennsboro Electric Co.went on strike today .

B. Write the correct abbreviation for each word.

1. Tuesday ____[Tues.]____   6. August ____[Aug.]____

2. liter ____[l]____   7. Avenue ____[Ave.]____

3. Captain ____[Capt.]____   8. foot ____[ft]____

4. pint ____[pt]____   9. Wednesday ____[Wed.]____

5. Mister ____[Mr.]____   10. inch ____[in.]____

C. Add commas where needed. Use the proofreading symbol (≡) under letters that should be capitalized.

1. our first three presidents were washington, adams, and jefferson.

2. on september 17, 1796, washington delivered his famous farewell address.

3. "do not count your chickens before they are hatched," said aesop.

4. yes, the dead sea is the saltiest.

5. do you want a sandwich, dan?

D. Add exclamation points, question marks, and apostrophes where needed.

1. Hurrah!The storm is over.

2. How much damage did it do ?

3. Im going to help our neighbors.

4. My fathers house was not damaged.

5. What a terrible twenty minutes that was !

E. Add quotation marks where needed.

1. "Have you read *Oliver Twist* by Dickens?" asked Colleen.

2. "No," said Martina, "but I would like to read it."

3. "Will you tell me about it?" she asked.

4. "Oliver," said Colleen, "was a poor orphan boy."

5. She continued, "He became involved with criminals in London."

F. Add quotation marks or underlining where needed.

1. Charles Dickens also wrote the novel <u>Great Expectations</u>.

2. Estelle in the television show "Ideals" loves that book.

3. She also appreciates great art, such as the <u>Mona Lisa</u>.

4. "Death Be Not Proud" is her favorite poem.

5. Estelle wrote her short story "Awaken" based on it.

Try It Yourself

Write four sentences about one of your favorite books.
Be sure to use capital letters and punctuation marks correctly.

_____

_____

_____

_____

Check Your Own Work

Choose a selection from your writing portfolio, your journal, a work in progress, an assignment from another class, or a letter. Revise it, applying the skills you have reviewed. The checklist will help you.

✔ Do your sentences end with the right punctuation marks?

✔ Have you followed the rules for commas?

✔ Have you used apostrophes and quotation marks correctly?

✔ Have you capitalized all proper nouns and proper adjectives?

Name _____

128. Using Homophones

> **Homophones** are words that sound alike, may be spelled differently, and have different meanings.
> For example, *sent*, *cent*, and *scent* are homophones.

Write on each line the correct word from the group of homophones.

blue	seen	flour	site	would
blew	scene	flower	sight	wood

weigh	herd	son	time	fare
way	heard	sun	thyme	fair

1. The county ___[fair]___ will begin on Saturday.

2. I have my bus ___[fare]___ ready.

3. What a ___[sight]___ it will be!

4. This year the ___[site]___ is Lake Hauto Park.

5. Mikey ___[heard]___ that there are buffalo in that park.

6. Yes, there is a small ___[herd]___.

7. Have you actually ___[seen]___ the buffalo?

8. Yes, they create a beautiful ___[scene]___.

9. There's still ___[time]___ to enter the baking contest.

10. I will make biscuits and season them with ___[thyme]___.

11. How much ___[flour]___ does one batch require?

12. Cathy carved our state ___[flower]___ for the contest.

13. The ___[way]___ she carves will bring her honors.

14. Her large sculpture does not ___[weigh]___ much.

15. What type of ___[wood]___ does she use?

16. I ___[would]___ like to buy some.

17. Is ___[sun]___ predicted for Saturday?

18. Nadine's ___[son]___ said that it is.

19. When Saturday came, the sky was ___[blue]___.

20. A slight breeze ___[blew]___ over the fair.

129. Recognizing Antonyms

> **Antonyms** are words that are opposite in meaning. For example, *softly* and *loudly* are antonyms.

A. Underline the two words in each sentence that are opposite in meaning.

1. His former <u>enemy</u> became his best <u>friend</u>.
2. Mr. Smith raised his <u>disciplined</u> voice and calmed the <u>unruly</u> crowd.
3. The <u>innocent</u> sometimes suffer for the <u>guilty</u>.
4. Roses are <u>scarce</u> in winter, but they are <u>plentiful</u> in summer.
5. I saw two <u>industrious</u> ants and one <u>lazy</u> one.
6. The <u>ugly</u> duckling became a <u>beautiful</u> swan.
7. The elevator <u>ascended</u> to the sixth floor and then <u>descended</u> to the basement.
8. The girls ran <u>quickly</u>, but the boys walked <u>slowly</u>.
9. Everybody admires a <u>courteous</u> person but not a <u>rude</u> one.
10. A cloudy day is <u>dull</u>, while a sunny one is <u>bright</u>.

B. Complete each sentence with an antonym of the *italicized* word.

1. Monica has been *present* four days and _____[absent]_____ one day.
2. *Cold* drinks are refreshing in _____[hot]_____ weather.   **[Answers will vary.**
3. Rise *early*, and you will not be _____[late]_____ for the trip.   **Samples are given.]**
4. Cotton is a leading *export* of the United States, while coffee is a major _____[import]_____.
5. *Above* the bridge soared an airplane, while _____[below]_____ the bridge glided a pleasure boat.
6. This box is *empty*, but that one is _____[full]_____.
7. A *narrow* lane led to the _____[wide]_____ highway.
8. This bread is *fresh*, but those buns are _____[stale]_____.
9. The instructor *asked* the question, and Michael _____[answered]_____ it promptly.
10. The hare moved *quickly*, but the turtle crawled along _____[slowly]_____.

130. Identifying Synonyms

Synonyms are words that have the same general meaning.
For example, *guard*, *defend*, and *protect* are synonyms.

Below each sentence, cross out the word that is not a synonym
for the *italicized* word.

1. Aladdin traveled with his *friends.*
   companions   ~~enemies~~   comrades   associates

2. The rider immediately realized his *peril.*
   danger   risk   ~~mistake~~   hazard

3. *Glistening* coins made up his valuable collection.
   bright   sparkling   glittering   ~~rare~~

4. Our journey may prove *tedious.*
   ~~profitable~~   irksome   tiresome   wearisome

5. King Midas was a *foolish* man.
   unwise   rash   ~~sensible~~   stupid

6. Jeremy *answered* without hesitation.
   replied   responded   retorted   ~~reacted~~

7. Our parents try to *protect* us.
   defend   ~~encourage~~   safeguard   shield

8. Zachary was always a *happy* lad.
   jolly   cheerful   joyous   ~~generous~~

9. A loud cry *frightened* the animal.
   ~~awakened~~   terrified   alarmed   startled

10. The judge showed *mercy* toward the prisoner.
    compassion   clemency   ~~cruelty~~   pity

Name_____

131. Recognizing the Exact Meaning of Words

Although synonyms have the same general meaning, there is often a slight difference that makes one word better than another in a sentence.

In each sentence circle the better word from the pair of synonyms.

1a. The French Revolution (lasted continued) approximately ten years.

1b. Unrest, however, (lasted continued) for decades.

2a. The Revolution was caused by a (bankrupt depleted) treasury.

2b. France was (bankrupt depleted) when King Louis XVI came to the throne.

3a. In 1789 the king (called summoned) the States-General, or national assembly.

3b. Three groups, estates, were (called summoned) together to raise money.

4a. The king and his advisors secretly formed a (plot plan) against the reforms.

4b. The people of Paris were outraged when they learned of his (plot plan).

5a. On July 14th they (invaded stormed) the Bastille, a lightly defended prison.

5b. In October a mob (invaded stormed) the royal palace at Versailles.

6a. In June 1791 the king and his family tried to (escape flee) France.

6b. The king's trying to (escape flee) was viewed as treasonous.

7a. A National Convention wrote a constitution for the (country republic).

7b. Members of the convention declared France a (country republic).

8a. The king was (beheaded executed) for betraying his country.

8b. Queen Marie Antoinette was (beheaded executed) in the same manner.

9a. After the overthrow of the monarchy, the Reign of Terror (commenced began).

9b. The government (commenced began) a regime of executions of suspected enemies.

10a. Maximilien François Marie Isidore de Robespierre (led governed) the Reign of Terror.

10b. At that time the National Convention (led governed) as a dictatorship.

Name_____

132. Using Action Verbs

> Writing can be improved by using verbs that describe actions clearly and vividly.

A. Complete each sentence with a synonym for *went.* **[Possible answers are given.]**

strolled	scurried	galloped	glided	floated
jumped	trotted	swerved	marched	ambled
bounded	tiptoed	hobbled	hopped	cruised

1. The band ____[marched]____ down State Street.

2. A clown ____[tiptoed]____ up to an unsuspecting child.

3. Two decorated horses ____[trotted]____ next to the police's float.

4. The largest float ____[glided]____ down the middle of the street.

5. A mother and her child ____[strolled]____ along with the parade.

6. The baton twirlers ____[bounded]____ along the street.

7. The colorful balloons ____[floated]____ up into the air.

8. A man on stilts ____[hobbled]____ behind the horses.

9. A convertible with the mayor inside ____[cruised]____ down the street.

10. The ice cream man ____[ambled]____ up the sidewalk.

11. Suddenly a horse ____[galloped]____ to the front of the parade.

12. A float at the front ____[swerved]____ to avoid a collision.

13. A police officer ____[scurried]____ to see what was the problem.

14. A cat ____[jumped]____ up on the rear of the first float.

15. With all the noise, it ____[hopped]____ off.

B. Complete each sentence with a synonym for *rang.* **[Possible answers are given.]**

| chimed | tolled | tinkled | jingled | pealed |

1. The bell ____[tinkled]____ in the light wind.

2. Sleigh bells ____[jingled]____ merrily.

3. The clock ____[chimed]____ the hour.

4. The bell ____[tolled]____ for the funeral.

5. Wedding bells ____[pealed]____ in the bell tower.

133. Using Colorful Adjectives

> Writing can be improved by substituting colorful adjectives for dull, colorless ones.

A. Complete each sentence with a synonym for *good*. [Possible answers are given.]

interesting   excellent   enjoyable   correct   resourceful

1. My mom is a ___[resourceful]___ person.
2. She makes ___[interesting]___ crafts.
3. She does ___[excellent]___ work.
4. Mom uses the ___[correct]___ tools.
5. I have an ___[enjoyable]___ day helping her.

B. Complete each sentence with a synonym for *big*. [Possible answers are given.]

spacious   huge   enormous   large   roomy
towering   grand   vast   immense   tall

1. Modern architects erect ___[towering]___ buildings.
2. The man became heir to a ___[vast]___ estate.
3. A ___[huge]___ elephant led the parade.
4. In the park stood an ___[immense]___ statue of Napoleon.
5. My uncle is a ___[tall]___ man.
6. The wind has carved that ___[enormous]___ rock into fantastic shapes.
7. The royal guests used the ___[grand]___ staircase.
8. The hiking boots were too ___[large]___ for her tiny feet.
9. My brother's sweater is quite ___[roomy]___ on me.
10. The room was ___[spacious]___ enough for two beds.

C. Complete each sentence with a synonym for *pretty*. [Possible answers are given.]

beautiful   becoming   attractive   picturesque   delicate

1. She wore a ___[becoming]___ hat to the wedding.
2. Before the altar stood a vase of ___[delicate]___ flowers.
3. The bride and groom were photographed before the ___[beautiful]___ sunset.
4. Ruth described the ___[picturesque]___ scene to her friends.
5. The decorations at the reception were very ___[attractive]___.

134. Rewriting Rambling Sentences

Writing is dull and hard to follow when too many long sentences are strung together with *and*. Revise such sentences by dividing them into shorter sentences.

Rewrite each sentence into shorter, more concise sentences. **[Possible answers are given.]**

1. Christopher Houston Carson was nicknamed Kit Carson and he was a trapper, a guide, a military scout, an Indian agent, a soldier, and a rancher.

   [Christopher Houston Carson was nicknamed

   Kit Carson. He was a trapper, a guide, a military

   scout, an Indian agent, a soldier, and a rancher.]

2. He was born in Madison County, Kentucky, and it was Christmas Eve and it was 1809 and he was the ninth of fourteen children.

   [He was born in Madison County, Kentucky, on Christmas Eve in 1809. He was the ninth

   of fourteen children.]

3. His dad died when he was young and so he went to work as an apprentice to a saddle-and-harness maker.

   [His dad died when he was young. So he went to work as an apprentice to a

   saddle-and-harness maker.]

4. He ran away from home in 1826 and he went with a wagon train full of hunters and they were going to Santa Fe.

   [He ran away from home in 1826 with a wagon train full of hunters. They were going

   to Santa Fe.]

CONTINUED

Revising a Paragraph

143

5. He was nineteen and he became a fur trapper and he led fur-trapping expeditions in the mountains of the West.

   [When he was nineteen, he became a fur trapper. He led fur-trapping expeditions in the

   mountains of the West.]

6. While he was trapping, he got to know the Native Americans and he was honest and he was courageous.

   [While he was trapping, he got to know the Native Americans. He was honest and courageous.]

7. He learned the ways of the Native Americans and he learned their history and his first two wives were Native Americans.

   [He learned the ways and history of the Native Americans. His first two wives were

   Native Americans.]

8. He was the hunter for a fort and the fort was in Colorado and he guided an explorer named John C. Frémont to California.

   [He was the hunter for a fort in Colorado. He guided an explorer named John C. Frémont

   to California.]

9. Frémont wrote in a diary and Frémont wrote about Kit Carson in the diary and Kit Carson became a national hero.

   [Frémont wrote about Kit Carson in a diary. Kit Carson became a national hero.]

10. He became a rancher in New Mexico and he became a soldier in the Civil War and people wrote books about him that made him a legend.

    [He became a rancher in New Mexico and a soldier in the Civil War. People wrote books

    about him that made him a legend.]

Kit Carson had the interest and courage to do many different things during his life. Name some of the things you are interested in doing. Do you need courage to do them?

135. Letter Writing

A friendly letter has five parts:
heading — contains the address of the writer and the date of the letter
salutation — the greeting
body — contains the message
complimentary close — the farewell
signature — the name of the writer

A. Use the proofreading symbol (≡) to indicate which letters should be capitalized. Add punctuation where needed.

1754 peachtree street
atlanta, ga 30309
june 11, 2003

dear patricia ,

B. Add punctuation to the letter where needed.
Use the proofreading symbol (≡) to indicate capitalization.

217 parker avenue
new london, ct 06320
november 18, 2003

dear grandmother ,

thanksgiving is almost here, and i can hardly wait to visit you. mother
asked me to tell you that we shall arrive the day before. maybe
granddad will meet us at the corner .

already i have visions of delicious turkey and pumpkin pies. remind
uncle adam that he promised to take us to the football game in
the afternoon .

i like school very much this year. you will be proud of me when i show
you my papers. i'll bring my report card with me .

your grandson ,
michael

136. Letter Writing

In thank-you letters, you should mention the gift and the reason you like it.

In the following letter all the parts run together. Copy the letter with each part in its proper place. Add capital letters and punctuation where needed.

194 juniper drive levittown pennsylvania 19056 january 8 2003 dear aunt sara i have been wishing for a set of pastels for such a long time how did you know that i wanted a set there is an art course coming up in the spring that i would like to attend i shall use them there you have made me so happy thank you very much your loving niece heidi

[194 Juniper Drive]

[Levittown, PA 19056]

[January 8, 2003]

[Dear Aunt Sara,]

[I have been wishing for a set of pastels for such a long time. How did you know that I wanted a set? There is an art course coming up in the spring that I would like to attend. I shall use them there. You have made me so happy. Thank you very much.]

[Your loving niece,]

[Heidi]

Name _____

137. Using the Internet: Surfing the Web

One reason for using the Internet is to do research. Generally, to do so you need to "surf" the World Wide Web. That means you move through the Internet, looking at sites and checking pages to find the information you want.

Here are some things to remember about surfing:

1. **Never give your or your family's personal information over the Internet.**

Keep personal details, such as address and telephone number, to yourself. Talk to your teacher or a parent before you post something on the Internet.

2. **Narrow your keywords, or search words, as much as you can.**

The more on target your keywords are, the more quickly you should be able to find information.

3. **Keep your mind and your efforts on the topic you are researching.**

There is a great amount of information on the Internet. Do not get sidetracked by something interesting that is not directly related to the topic you are researching. Keep reminding yourself of what you are looking for. This will help you focus on your search. If you don't stay focused, your research may take more time than it should, or you may not find what you are looking for.

4. **Use good Internet manners.**
   - Make sure your posted messages are clear so that they can be easily understood.
   - Don't shout! Writing messages in capital letters is called shouting. Use capital letters only for titles or to emphasize something special.

5. **Check all facts you get from the Internet.**

You cannot believe everything you find on the Internet. Some information may be out of date. Some may be just wrong. Generally, you can trust government, education, and most business sites. Compare the information from the Internet with other sources or check with an adult.

You are looking for information about George Washington as commander-in-chief of the Continental Army. Think about each situation described here. What should you do?

1. You find some information on the White House home page about George Washington.

   Would you probably use it? __[Yes]_____

   Why? __[The White House is part of the federal government, so it is a reliable source. The

   information must relate to George Washington as commander-in-chief of the Continental Army

   during the Revolutionary War, not Washington as president.]

2. One Internet site looks as though it has just the information you need. To gain access to it, you must type your name, address, and telephone number.

   Would you do this? __[No]_____

   Why? __[Students should know never to give personal information over the Internet.]

   _____

3. You are trying to think of keywords that will help you find the information you want.

   List two keywords or phrases you might try. __[Possible answers: "Continental Army,"

   General Washington, "commander-in-chief Washington"

   If students enter only commander-in-chief, they will be given sites relating to all presidents.]

4. You find an Internet site where you are able to send an e-mail to a park ranger at Valley Forge National Park. However, you do not think she is giving you the information you are requesting. How can you let her know this? Put a check mark by the best answer.

   _____ a. By typing her a message in all capital letters to get her attention

   __[✔]__ b. By restating your question so that she can understand it better

   _____ c. By asking the question again in exactly the same way that you asked it the first time

   [Choice a is the opposite of good manners on the Internet.
   Choice c is not a sensible action because the ranger did not understand
   the question the first time.]

138. Using an Encyclopedia: Main Ideas and Details

Encyclopedias are important sources for research. In addition to the main encyclopedia **entry** for a topic, you may find a **list of related sources** at the end of an article. These are additional resources for you to check. Some encyclopedias also have **index volumes** that cross-reference words within the encyclopedia that are related to each entry. Other encyclopedias list questions to help you pick out the most important information in an entry.

How can you organize all the information you find? One way is to make notes about what you read for use later when you begin to write your paper. Look for main ideas (topics) and supporting details as you read the encyclopedia entries.

Encyclopedia entries often have clues to help you find the main idea such as main-idea phrases in bold type or an outline at the end of an article. As you look at a particular encyclopedia article in a printed volume, on a CD-ROM, or on-line, note how it is organized to help you.

Suppose you are looking for information about astronaut John Herschel Glenn, Jr. After reading an encyclopedia article about him, you might see that you could divide your notes into three parts. Each part would be about a period in his life. You would have three main ideas, each followed by subtopics and details. Look at this outline.

John Herschel Glenn, Jr.

I. Glenn's early life

  A. Education

      1. Muskingum College—1939–1942

      2. Classes at University of Maryland—B.S. in 1962

  B. Marine Corps

      1. World War II—59 missions as a pilot in the Pacific area

      2. Korean War—90 missions; earned 5 Distinguished Flying Crosses and 19 Air Medals

      3. Became test pilot—set speed record from Los Angeles to New York City in 3 hours 25 minutes

II. Glenn as an astronaut

The second main idea would deal with him as an astronaut, with details of his work with NASA, and so on.

The last main idea could be about his later career in politics and government service. It would provide details of the offices he held and the work he did.

CONTINUED

Name_____

Pick a well-known person in science, government, or another area.
Find an encyclopedia article about the person. Read it and take notes,
making sure to list the main ideas and details in an outline as you
work. Look for clues in the entry to help you organize your work.

I. [Answers will vary depending on the choice of subject. Check that students have identified

   A. the most important information about their subject and provided several details to explain

      1. and support those ideas. Students should include at least two listings at each outline level:

      2. I and II, A and B, 1. and 2.]

_____

_____

_____

_____

_____

_____

_____

_____

_____

_____

_____

_____

_____

_____

_____

_____

_____

_____

_____

Name_____

139. Using an Almanac

Almanacs are fascinating reference books full of facts. Almanacs are published every year and give up-to-date information on a variety of topics. For example, you can find a list of important events in the history of U.S. spaceflight from 1961 to the present. You also can find answers to questions such as What are the 10 largest cities in the United States or in the world?

Almanacs generally have both a contents listing and an index. To find information, decide on a keyword or phrase about your topic and then look for it in the index. For example, if you are interested in rail travel in the United States, you might use **railroads** as your keyword and when you find railroads, then look for **U.S.**

Information in an almanac is often given as a table, chart, or list. There is less background information in an almanac than you will find in an encyclopedia.

Research Skills

The Great Lakes

Source: National Ocean Service, U.S. Dept. of Commerce

The Great Lakes form the world's largest body of fresh water, and with their connecting waterways are the largest inland water transportation unit. Draining the great North Central basin of the U.S., they enable shipping to reach the Atlantic via their outlet, the St. Lawrence R., and to reach the Gulf of Mexico via the Illinois Waterway, from Lake Michigan to the Mississippi R. A 3d outlet connects with the Hudson R. and then the Atlantic via the New York State Barge Canal System. Traffic on the Illinois Waterway and the N.Y. State Barge Canal System is limited to recreational boating and small shipping vessels.

Only one of the lakes, Lake Michigan, is wholly in the U.S.; the others are shared with Canada. Ships move from the shores of Lake Superior to Whitefish Bay at the E end of the lake, then through the Soo (Sault Ste. Marie) locks, through the St. Mary's R. and into Lake Huron. To reach Gary and the Port of Indiana and South Chicago, IL, ships move W from Lake Huron to Lake Michigan through the Straits of Mackinac. Lake Superior is 601 ft above low water datum at Rimouski, Quebec, on the International Great Lakes Datum (1985). From Duluth, MN, to the E end of Lake Ontario is 1,156 mi.

	Superior	Michigan	Huron	Erie	Ontario
Length in mi	350	307	206	241	193
Breadth in mi	160	118	183	57	53
Deepest soundings in ft	1,333	923	750	210	802
Volume of water in cu mi	2,935	1,180	850	116	393
Area (sq mi) water surface—U.S.	20,600	22,300	9,100	4,980	3,560
Canada	11,100	.....	13,900	4,930	3,990
Area (sq mi) entire drainage basin—U.S.	16,900	45,600	16,200	18,000	15,200
Canada	32,400	.....	35,500	4,720	12,100
TOTAL AREA (sq mi) U.S. and Canada	**81,000**	**67,900**	**74,700**	**32,630**	**34,850**
Low water datum above mean water level at Rimouski, Quebec, avg. level in ft (1985)	601.10	577.50	577.50	569.20	243.30
Latitude, N	46° 25 min	41° 37 min	43° 00 min	41° 23 min	43° 11 min
	49° 00 min	46° 06 min	46° 17 min	42° 52 min	44° 15 min
Longitude, W	84° 22 min	84° 45 min	79° 43 min	78° 51 min	76° 03 min
	92° 06 min	88° 02 min	84° 45 min	83° 29 min	79° 53 min
National boundary line in mi	282.8	None	260.8	251.5	174.6
United States shoreline (mainland only) mi	863	1,400	580	431	300

Study the sample almanac entry on page 151. Then answer the following questions.

Research Skills

1. What is the topic of this entry? _____ [The Great Lakes] _____

2. How many lakes are listed? _____ [five] _____

3. List the lakes in order from the one with the largest total area in square miles to the one with the smallest total area in square miles.

   _____ [Lake Superior, about 81,000 sq mi] _____

   _____ [Lake Huron, about 74,700 sq mi] _____

   _____ [Lake Michigan, about 67,900 sq mi] _____

   _____ [Lake Ontario, about 34,850 sq mi] _____

   _____ [Lake Erie, about 32,630 sq mi] _____

4. Which lake has the longest United States shoreline?

   _____ [Lake Michigan] _____

5. About how long is this lake's shoreline? _____ [about 1,400 miles] _____

6. Only one lake is completely in the United States. Which one is it?

   _____ [Lake Michigan] _____

7. If you needed to find one of the lakes on a map, what information in this entry would you use to help you find the lake?

   _____ [latitude and longitude] _____

What might be the best keyword or phrase to use when looking up information in an almanac to answer the following questions? [Answers may vary. Sample answers are given.]

8. What tourist attractions can be found in Washington, D.C., the capital of the United States?

   _____ [Washington, D.C.; U.S. capital; sightseeing in Washington, D.C.; tourist attractions in Washington, D.C.] _____

9. What is the monthly normal temperature in January for Anchorage, Alaska?

   _____ [meteorology, weather, temperatures] _____

10. Which state had the lowest population density per square mile in 1990?

   _____ [U.S. population, population by state, population density] _____

Name_____

140. Using an Atlas: Physical and Political Maps

An **atlas** is a book of maps that you may use to research certain types of geographical information. An atlas may contain maps of continents, countries, states, and even large cities.

The maps in an atlas have different purposes. For example, a **political map** shows boundaries of states and countries. It also shows cities. A **physical map** shows information about rivers, elevation above sea level, and other natural features of the earth. A **natural resources map** shows the location of things like oil, coal, forests, and farmland.

The **map key,** or **legend**, tells what the different symbols on the map mean. The **map scale** tells the size of the map in relation to the actual distance. A scale may show that 1 inch represents 800 miles. You can use a map scale to find the distance between places.

Look at the map below that shows New Mexico and Texas.

Notice the information in the map key and then locate the map scale.

Name_____

Study the map on page 153. Then answer these questions.

In which state can you find the following cities?

1. Abilene _____[Texas]_____   2. Albuquerque ___[New Mexico]___

3. Amarillo _____[Texas]_____   4. Alamogordo _____[New Mexico]___

5. Santa Fe ____[New Mexico]____   6. Corpus Christi_____[Texas]_____

7. What is the state capital of Texas? _____[Austin]_____

8. What is the state capital of New Mexico? _____[Albuquerque]_____

9. In which states do you find the Pecos River?
_____[New Mexico and Texas]_____

10 In which state do you find the Trinity River?
_____[Texas]_____

11. In which state do you find the Rio Grande?
_____[New Mexico]_____

12. What forms the border between Texas and Mexico?
_____[Rio Grande]_____

13. In which state do you find the Sacramento Mountains?
_____[New Mexico]_____

14. In which state do you find the Edwards Plateau?
_____[Texas]_____

About how many miles is it between the following cities?

15. Fort Worth and San Antonio ____[about 250 miles]_____

16. Carlsbad and Gallup ____[about 340 miles]_____

17. Taos and Albuquerque ____[about 100 miles]_____

18. Dallas and Houston ____[about 225 miles]_____

19. Midland and El Paso ____[about 300 miles]_____

20. Amarillo and Las Cruces ____[about 350 miles]_____

Sentence Diagrams

A diagram is a visual outline of a sentence. It shows the essential parts of the sentence *(subject, verb, object, complement)* and the relationship of the other words and constructions to those essentials.

Diagramming a Simple Sentence

A. A simple sentence has one complete thought. This simple sentence has one subject noun, one verb, and one direct object.

Yesterday many excited children played noisy games in the park.

Here's how to diagram it.

1. The main line of a diagram is a horizontal line.

   _____

2. The verb in the sentence is *played*. Write *played* on the center of the diagram line.

   _____ played _____

3. Who played? Children played. *Children* is the subject. Write *children* on the line in front of *played*. Draw a vertical line to separate *children* and *played*. The vertical line should cut through the horizontal line.

   _____ children | played _____

4. Whom or what did the children play? They played games. *Games* is the direct object. Write *games* on the line after *played*. Draw a vertical line to separate *played* and *games*. This vertical line should touch the horizontal line but not cut through it.

   _____ children | played | games _____

CONTINUED

5. To find the modifiers of the verb, ask the questions *how, when, where, why*. Played when? Played *yesterday*. Played where? Played *in the park*. Write the modifiers on slanted lines under the verb. Note how the prepositional phrase is written.

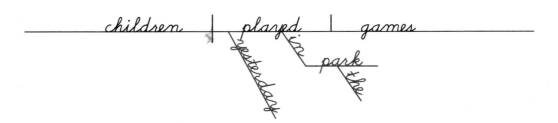

6. To find the modifiers of the subject, ask the questions *what, what kind, how many, whose*. How many children? *Many* children. What kind of children? *Excited* children. Write each modifier on a slanted line under the subject.

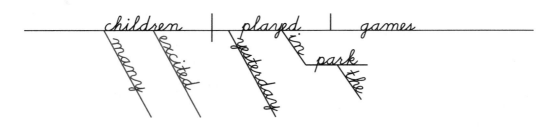

7. To find the modifiers of the object, ask the same questions you asked about the subject. Write each modifier on a slanted line under the object.

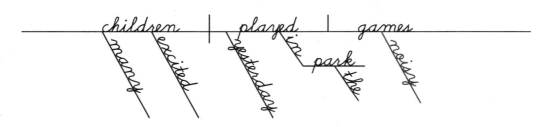

B. This simple sentence has a subject complement. Indicate a subject complement by drawing a slanted line pointing back to the subject between the verb and the complement. Remember that the complement can be a noun, a pronoun, or an adjective.

Mrs. Mitchell is a good teacher.

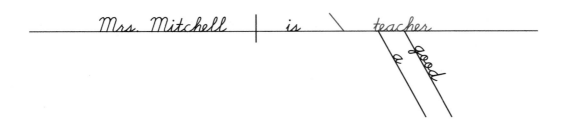

C. This simple sentence has a compound subject. Subjects must always appear on horizontal lines. Place the subject on parallel lines and write the conjunction on a broken line between the words it joins.

Tom and Pepe played tennis yesterday.

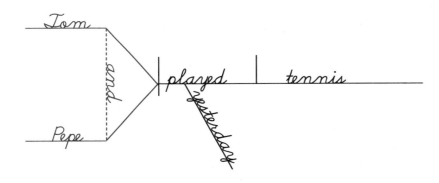

D. This simple sentence has a compound verb. Indicate a compound verb the same way as a compound subject.

Ned raked and bagged the leaves.

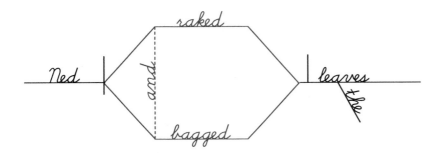

CONTINUED

Sentence Diagrams

Try It Yourself

Diagram each of these sentences on a sheet of paper.

1. A severe storm completely ruined the beautiful garden near our garage.
2. Carol was the winner of the first prize.
3. Lewis and Clark bravely explored the mountains of the West.
4. The helpful children washed and polished the old silverware.
5. The creaking old house was extremely scary.

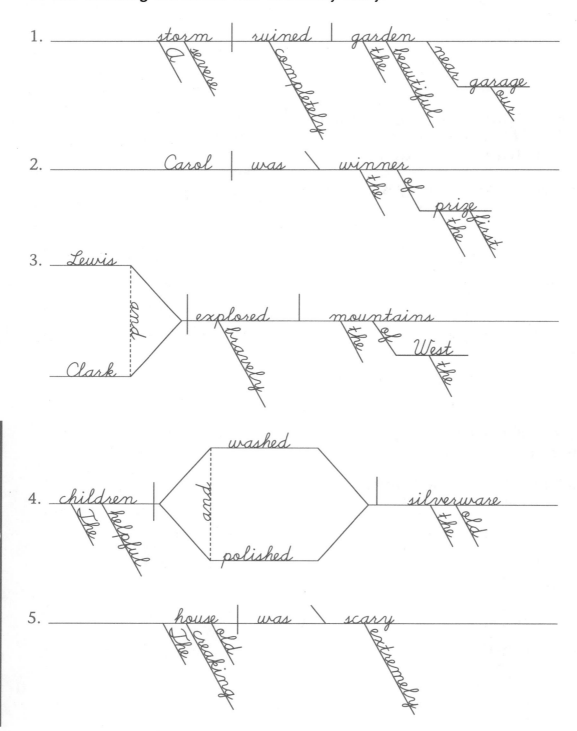

Handbook of Terms

A

adjective A word that describes a noun or pronoun.

Some descriptive adjectives come from proper nouns and are called proper adjectives. A proper adjective begins with a capital letter: *American* history.

The adjectives *a, an,* and *the* point out nouns. They are called articles. *See also* **articles.**

Demonstrative adjectives point out specific persons, places, or things.

- *This* and *that* point out one person, place, or thing.
- *These* and *those* point out more than one person, place, or thing.
- *This* and *these* point out persons, places, or things that are near.
- *That* and *those* point out persons, places, or things that are far.

Possessive adjectives show possession or ownership. The possessive adjectives are *my, your, his, her, its, our, your,* and *their.*

Possessive adjectives should not be confused with contractions that sound the same or almost the same. *Its, your,* and *there* are possessive adjectives. *It's, you're,* and *they're* are contractions.

Some adjectives tell exactly how many: *ten, twenty-five, third, twelfth.*

Some adjectives tell about how many: *many, few, several, some.*

An adjective usually comes before the noun it modifies: *sunny* morning, *hot* chocolate.

An adjective that follows a verb of being is a subject complement. A subject complement completes the meaning of the verb and describes the subject of the sentence: The night was *dark* and *cold.*

Some words may function as nouns or adjectives: *drama, drama* class, *property, property* tax.

See also **comparison.**

adverb A word that modifies a verb, an adjective, or another adverb.

An adverb of time answers the question *when* or *how often:* It rained *yesterday.* We *usually* eat lunch at noon.

An adverb of place answers the question *where:* Toshi bent his head *forward.* Sit *here* by the gate.

An adverb of manner answers the question *how* or *in what manner:* Jason draws *well.* She dances the waltz *gracefully.*

A negative idea is expressed by using one negative word. This negative word may be *no, not, none, never,* or *nothing.* These words should be used only in sentences that have no other negative words: I do *not* have any (not *no*) apples.

See also **comparison.**

antonyms Words that are opposite in meaning: *smooth* and *rough, soft* and *hard.*

apostrophe A punctuation mark (') used to show ownership: the *cook's* hat, the *girls'* horses.

An apostrophe is used to replace letters left out in a contraction: *wasn't* for *was not; I'm* for *I am.*

articles The adjectives *a, an,* and *the.* They point out nouns.

A and *an* are indefinite articles. An indefinite article refers to any of a class of things. *A* is used before words beginning with a consonant sound. *An* is used before words beginning with a vowel sound: *a* banana, *an* elephant.

The is the definite article. The definite article refers to one or more specific things: *the* bananas in *the* bowl, *the* elephants in *the* zoo.

C

capitalization The use of capital letters. Capital letters are used for many purposes, including the following:

- the first word of a sentence: *The* bell rang.
- an abbreviation if the word it stands for begins with a capital letter: *Rev.* for *Reverend.*
- the first word and the name of a person addressed in the salutation of a letter: *Dear Marie,*
- the first word in the complimentary close of a letter: *Yours truly,*
- the principal words in the titles of books, plays, pictures, and most poems: *A Tale of Two Cities, Romeo and Juliet, Mona Lisa,* "*Fire and Ice*"
- the first word of a direct quotation: Mother said, "*It's* time for my favorite television program."

- proper nouns: *United States*
- North, East, South, West when they refer to a section of the country or the world: the old *West*. They are not capitalized when they refer to direction: He drove *west* on Main Street.
- the pronoun *I,* the interjection *O*
- names referring to deities or to sacred books: *God,* the *Bible*
- two-letter state postal abbreviations: *MA, NY, CA*

comma A punctuation mark (,) used to make reading clearer. Among its many uses are the following:

- to separate words or groups of words in a series: elephants, giraffes, hyenas, and monkeys
- to set off parts of dates, addresses, or geographical names: January 1, 2003; 321 Spring Road, Atlanta, Georgia; Paris, France
- to set off words in direct address: Josie, I'm so pleased that you called me this morning.
- after the words *yes* and *no* when they introduce sentences: Yes, I agree with you completely.
- to set off direct quotations, unless a question mark or exclamation point is required: "We have only vanilla and chocolate today," he said in an apologetic tone.
- to separate simple sentences connected by the conjunctions *and, but,* and *or:* She called his name, but he didn't answer her.
- after the salutation and closing in a social or friendly letter: Dear Mrs. Porter, Dear Ben, Sincerely yours,

comparison The act of comparing. Many adjectives can be used to compare two or more persons, places, or things.

- An adjective in the *positive* degree describes one or more persons, places, or things: The cat is *quiet.* The dogs are *powerful.*
- An adjective in the comparative degree compares two persons, places, or things. Form comparative adjectives by adding *-er* to the positive degree or by putting *more* before the positive degree: The cat is *quieter* than the dog. The dog is *more powerful* than the cat.
- An adjective in the superlative degree compares three or more persons, places, or things. Form superlative adjectives by adding *-est* to the positive degree or by putting *most* before the positive degree: Cats are the *quietest* animals I know. That dog is the *most powerful* animal in the neighborhood.

(continued on next page)

The comparative *fewer* refers to number; the comparative *less* refers to quantity: There are *fewer* apples than oranges. My car uses *less* gas than yours.

Like adjectives, adverbs have three degrees of comparison— positive, comparative, and superlative.

- Form the comparative degree by adding *-er* to the positive degree or by putting *more* before the positive degree: *faster, more carefully.*

- Form the superlative degree by adding *-est* to the positive degree or by putting *most* before the positive degree: *fastest, most carefully.*

compound subjects, predicates, objects In a simple sentence, the subject, the predicate, and the direct object may be compound.

- If a simple sentence has two or more simple subjects, it is said to have a compound subject: *Ivan* and *John* argued with the grocer.

- If a simple sentence has two or more verbs it is said to have a compound predicate: The baby *walks* and *talks* well.

- If a simple sentence has two or more direct objects, it is said to have a compound direct object: Wear your *hat, scarf,* and *gloves.*

conjunction A word used to connect words or groups of words. The most common conjunctions are *and, but,* and *or.* Conjunctions connect subject, predicates, direct objects, and sentences: Joshua *and* Leanne cut *and* pasted the words *and* pictures on the posters, *and* Nancy took orders.

contraction Two words written as one, with one or more letters omitted: *doesn't* for *does not, I've* for *I have.*

An apostrophe is used to show the omission of a letter or letters.

Subject pronouns are used with verbs to form contractions: *we're* for *we are, she's* for *she is.*

Some contractions and possessive pronouns sound alike or almost alike: *it's, its; you're, your.* They should not be confused.

D

direct object The direct object answers the question *whom* or *what* after an action verb in a sentence: Nathaniel gave the *baby* to his mother.

An object pronoun can be used as a direct object: Nathaniel gave *him* to his mother.

E

exclamation point A punctuation mark (!) used after an exclamatory sentence and after an exclamatory word or phrase: More than one thousand people attended the wedding! Wonderful! What a celebration!

H

homophones Words that sound alike but may be spelled differently and have different meanings: *sea* and *see*, *blue* and *blew.*

I

intensive pronoun An intensive pronoun ends in *-self* or *-selves.* The intensive pronouns are

myself	ourselves
yourself	yourselves
himself	themselves
herself	
itself	

Intensive pronouns are used for emphasis: She *herself* paid the bill.

interjection A word that expresses a strong feeling or emotion. An interjection is followed by an exclamation point: *Ouch! What! Oh!*

N

noun The name of a person, place, or thing.

There are two main kinds of nouns: proper nouns and common nouns.
- A common noun names any one member of a group of persons, places, or things: *queen, city, church.*
- A proper noun names a particular person, place, or thing. A proper noun is capitalized: *Queen Elizabeth, London, Westminster Abbey.*

A noun can be singular or plural.
- A singular noun names one person, place, or thing: *boy, river, berry.*
- A plural noun names more than one person, place, or thing: *boys, rivers, berries.*

(continued on next page)

The possessive form of a noun expresses possession or ownership. The apostrophe (') is the sign of a possessive noun.

- To form the possessive of a singular noun, add 's to the singular form: *architect's*
- To form the possessive of a plural noun that ends in *s*, add an apostrophe (') to the plural form: *farmers'*
- To form the possessive of a plural noun that does not end in *s*, add 's to the plural form: *children's*

O

order in a sentence The sequence of the subject and verb in a sentence expresses its order.

- When the verb in a sentence follows the subject, the sentence is in natural order: The *settlers planted* the seeds.
- When the main verb or the helping verb in a sentence comes before the subject, the sentence is in inverted order: Across the plain *marched* the tired *soldiers*.

P

period A punctuation mark (.) used at the end of a declarative or an imperative sentence and after initials and some abbreviations.

phrase A group of related words that forms a single unit within a sentence: *beside the sofa; before the storm.*

See also **prepositional phrases.**

possession Ownership.

possessive adjective *See* **adjective.**

possessive pronoun A pronoun that shows possession or ownership by the speaker; the person spoken to; or the person, place, or thing spoken about: *mine, yours, his, hers, its, ours,* and *theirs.*

Although possessive pronouns show ownership, they do not contain apostrophes: The new skates are *hers.*

predicate The part of a sentence that tells something about the subject. The predicate consists of a verb and its modifiers, objects, and complements, if any: Jason *laughed.* Nikki *ate breakfast.* They *have run through the tall grass.*

preposition A preposition is a word that relates a noun or a pronoun to some other word in the sentence. The noun or pronoun that follows the preposition is the object of the proposition: The huge mountain lion leaped *through* (preposition) the tall *grass* (object of the preposition).

- *Between* is used when speaking of two persons, places, or things; *among* is used when speaking of more than two.
- *From* is used when speaking of a person from whom something is received.
- *Off* means "away from." The expression *off of* is never correct.

prepositional phrase A phrase that is introduced by a preposition. A prepositional phrase contains a preposition and an object: *off* (preposition) the *grass* (object of the preposition).

An adjectival phrase is a prepositional phrase used as an adjective and modifies a noun: The cabin *in the woods* burned down.

An adverbial phrase is a prepositional phrase used as an adverb that modifies a verb: The river flows *into the sea.*

pronoun A word that takes the place of a noun or nouns.

A personal pronoun names

- the speaker (first person): *I, mine, me, we, ours, us*
- the person spoken to (second person): *you, yours*
- the person, place, or thing spoken about (third person): *he, she, it, his, hers, its, him, her, they, theirs, them*

A personal pronoun is singular when it refers to one person, place, or thing. A personal pronoun is plural when it refers to more than one person, place, or thing.

The third person singular pronoun can be masculine, feminine, or neuter.

A pronoun may be used as the subject of a sentence. The subject pronouns are *I, you, he, she, it, we,* and *they.*

A subject pronoun can replace a noun used as a subject complement.

A pronoun may be used as the direct object of a verb. The object pronouns are *me, you, him, her, it, us,* and *them.*

An object pronoun may be used as the object of a preposition.

See also **contraction, possessive pronoun, intensive pronoun,** *and* **reflexive pronoun.**

Q

question mark A punctuation mark (?) used at the end of a question: What time is it?

quotation marks Punctuation marks (" ") used before and after every direct quotation and every part of a divided quotation: "Let's go shopping," said Michiko. "I can go with you," Father said, "after I have eaten lunch."

(continued on next page)

Quotation marks enclose titles of short stories, poems, magazine articles, television shows, and radio programs. Titles of books, magazines, newspapers, movies, and works of art are usually printed in *italics* or are underlined. Television programs that are a continuing series are printed in *italics* or underlined.

R

reflexive pronoun A reflexive pronoun ends in *-self* or *-selves*. The reflexive pronouns are

myself	ourselves
yourself	yourselves
himself	themselves
herself	
itself	

A reflexive pronoun often refers to the subject of the sentence: She saw *herself* in the mirror.

S

sentence A group of words that expresses a complete thought.

A declarative sentence makes a statement; it is followed by a period: *The sun is shining.*

An interrogative sentence asks a question; it is followed by a question mark: *Where is my pen?*

An imperative sentence gives a command or makes a request; it is followed by a period: *Go to the store. Please pick up the papers.*

An exclamatory sentence expresses strong or sudden emotion; it is followed by an exclamation point: *What a loud noise that was!*

A sentence is made up of a subject and a predicate.

- The subject names a person, a place, or a thing about which a statement is made. The simple subject is a noun or pronoun without any of its modifiers: The *man* is riding.
- The complete subject is the simple subject with all its modifiers: *The tall, athletic young man* is riding his bike.
- The predicate tells something about the subject. The simple predicate is a verb without any of its modifiers, objects, and complements: Teresa *waved.*
- The complete predicate is the verb with all its modifiers, objects, and complements: Teresa *waved to the child from the window.*

A simple sentence contains one subject and one predicate. Either or both may be compound. *See also* **compound subjects, predicate, objects.**

See also **order in a sentence.**

subject The person, place, or thing that a sentence is about: *Daniel* spoke. The *prairie* was dry. The *cup* broke into pieces.

subject complement A word that completes the meaning of a linking verb in a sentence. A subject complement may be a noun, a pronoun, or an adjective: Broccoli is a green *vegetable*. The prettiest one was *she*. The sea will be *cold*.

synonyms Words with the same or almost the same meaning: *build, construct*.

V

verb A word that expresses action or being.

A verb has four principal parts: the present, the present participle, the past, and the past participle. A verb may be regular or irregular.

- The present participle is formed by adding *-ing* to the present.
- The simple past and past participle of regular verbs are formed by adding *-ed* or *-d* to the present.
- The simple past and past participle of irregular verbs are not formed by adding *-ed* or *-d* to the present.

The tense of a verb shows the time of its action.

- The simple present tense tells about an action that happens again and again: I *play* the piano every afternoon.
- The simple past tense tells about an action that happened in the past: I *played* the piano yesterday afternoon.
- The future tense tells about an action that will happen in the future; the future is formed with the present and the auxiliary verb *will:* I *will play* in the piano recital next Sunday.
- The present progressive tense tells what is happening now; the present progressive tense is formed with the present participle and a form of the verb *be:* He *is eating* his lunch now.
- The past progressive tense tells what was happening in the past; the past progressive tense is formed with the past participle and a past form of the verb *be:* He *was eating* his lunch when I saw him.

A transitive verb expresses an action that passes from a doer to a receiver. The receiver is the direct object of the verb: The dog *ate* the bone.

An intransitive verb has no receiver of the action. It does not have a direct object: The sun *shone* on the lake.

(continued on next page)

Handbook of Terms

An action verb is a word used to express action: The rabbit *hopped* across the grass.

A being verb is a word used to express existence. The most common being verbs are *is, are, was, were, be, being,* and *been:* The baby *was* hungry and fussy.

A linking verb links a subject with a subject complement (a noun, a pronoun, or an adjective). Verbs of being are linking verbs: She *is* a teacher. The winner *was* he. The children *will be* happy.

A verb phrase is a group of words that does the work of a single verb. A verb phrase contains one or more auxiliary or helping verbs *(is, are, has, have, will, can, could, would, should, etc.)* and a main verb: She *had forgotten* her hat.

A subject and a verb must always agree in number and person.

- Singular nouns and singular subject pronouns must have singular verbs. The third person singular of the simple present tense ends in *-s* or *-es:* I *run.* You *run.* He *runs.*

- Plural nouns and plural subject pronouns must have plural verbs. A plural verb does not end in *-s* or *-es:* We *run.* You *run.* They *run.*

- Use *am* with the first person singular subject pronoun: I *am* a soccer player.

- Use *is* with a singular noun or a third person singular subject pronoun: Paris *is* a city. She *is* a pianist. It *is* a truck.

- Use *are* with a plural noun, the second person subject pronoun, or a third person plural pronoun: Dogs *are* good pets. You *are* the winner. We *are* happy. They *are* my neighbors.

- Use *was* with a singular noun or a first or third person singular subject pronoun: The boy *was* sad. I *was* lucky. It *was* a hard job.

- Use *were* with a plural noun, a second person subject pronoun, or a third person plural subject pronoun: The babies *were* crying. You *were* a good friend.

- Use *doesn't* with a singular noun or a third person singular subject pronoun: He *doesn't* have a pencil. The teacher *doesn't* have a pen.

- Use *don't* with a plural noun, a second person subject pronoun, a first person plural subject pronoun, or a third person plural subject pronoun: Buses *don't* stop here. You *don't* have the tickets. We *don't* have to go.

The verb *lie (lie, lying, lay, lain)* means "to rest or recline." It is always intransitive: I *lay* down for a nap.

The verb *lay (lay, laying, laid, laid)* means "to put or place in position." It is always transitive: I *laid* the book on the desk.

The verb *sit (sit, sitting, sat, sat)* means "to have or keep a seat." It is always intransitive: The boy *sat* on the chair.

The verb *set (set, setting, set, set)* means "to place or to fix." It is always transitive: The boy *set* the package on the chair.

The verb *teach (teach, teaching, taught, taught)* means "to give instruction:" She *taught* me the song.

The verb *learn (learn, learning, learned, learned)* means "to receive instruction:" I *learned* the song.

The verb *let (let, letting, let, let)* means "to permit or allow:" They *let* us come along.

The verb *leave (leave, leaving, left, left)* means "to depart" or "to go away without taking:" They *left* us behind.

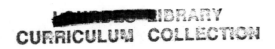